HOME GROWN LEADERS

Edgar J. Elliston

William Carey Library
Pasadena, California

Published by
William Carey Library
P.O. Box 40129
Pasadena, California 91114
(818) 798-0819

Library of Congress Cataloging-in-Publication Data

Elliston, Edgar J., 1943–

    Home grown leaders / by Edgar J. Elliston
        p.   cm.
    Includes bibliographical references.
    ISBN 0-87808-236-0 (pbk.)
    1. Christian leadership.   I. Title
BV652.1.E485   1992
253—dc20   92–61467
                                              CIP

Printed in the United States of America

CONTENTS

Contents

Contents

PREFACE

This book is intended for pastors and informed lay leaders as they seek to guide the emergence and development[1] of local church leaders.

The principles contained in this book have emerged from observing leadership development in both large urban churches and small rural churches in the U.S. and in Two-Thirds World contexts as diverse as Ethiopia, Kenya, Indonesia and Argentina.

The principles described in this book, while applied in the illustrations to lay leaders, also apply to the development of other kinds of leaders as well. Whether the person is a small group leader, a department head in a local church, a pastor or a denominational leader, the same principles apply to his/her development.

The purpose of this book is to describe an approach to multiply and equip effective and functioning local church leaders. The book seeks to show how to capitalize on an emerging trend among many large and rapidly growing churches of developing leaders in their own context not only for lay ministry roles, but for all of the levels or types of local church leadership. These leaders may serve on any level—not just as small group or lay leaders, but also as elders and pastors as well. The principles apply not only to mega-churches, but also to new or small churches regardless of their cultural or economic context. While these principles are widely used in charismatic and Pentecostal churches, many other non-Pentecostal churches are using them with the same effective results. The book is intended for pastors and other local leaders who are working in local churches to equip and enlist many new and developing leaders.

The approach suggested in this book may be used where resources are limited, where competence combined with spiritual maturity is desired and/or where a church is growing rapidly.

1

The leadership development methods described will lead to the development of leaders who fit their ministry contexts.

End Notes

1   "Leadership development" is to be distinguished from leadership "training" or "education." "Leadership development" is seen as a wholistic process which addresses both the broad equipping of the leader and his/her status/role relations within the leadership context. "Training" is understood to focus on the teaching of a person to function in a specific role. "Education" in this context is broader and less specific than training. Education, like training, acknowledges the followers and situation but does not, however, directly address either the situation or followers as part of the leadership developmental processes.

INTRODUCTION

What does a preaching elder in a small church in Great Bend, Kansas, have in common with the pastor of the Vision of the Future Church in Santa Fe, Argentina? Or, what does an Indonesian pastor of a small village church have in common with the pastor of a nomadic congregation among the pastoral Masai of Kenya? And, what do they all have in common with the pastor of a mega-church in southern California, Bangkok or Manila? What does the leader of a Pentecostal church in Santiago, Chile, have in common with a "mainline" denominational church in Columbus, Ohio? You are right if you responded, "the selection and development of local church leaders."

While the forms of leadership development vary, the need for leadership development demands attention wherever the church is. The needs for vision, guidance, motivation, coordination, and encouragement exist whenever Christians gather.

Many church leaders are interested in leadership development because of leadership problems they see in the churches they serve. Some who have been trained as "leaders" simply do not adequately function as "leaders." Too often their ministries prove to be dysfunctional for the churches they serve.

Pastors and informed lay leaders can address these and other problems as leadership development opportunities. Only a few of these problems will likely respond favorably to additional training. However, if the whole development process is considered, many of these issues are likely to move toward effective resolution.

Leadership development requires more than just training. This book describes one wholistic perspective of the process. Growing churches wherever they may be, whether in India, the Confederation of Independent States, Czechoslovakia or Canada, actively recruit and develop their own leaders. A trend among rapidly growing churches is the meeting of most of their leadership needs by "local" or "internal" leadership development processes. These leadership development processes focus on every kind of leader, including small group leaders through senior pastoral staff members. Hence, the interest in Home Grown Leaders. Local churches provide the primary arenas for identifying, selecting, and developing the whole range of Christian leaders. A person may attend a Christian college, university or seminary for a training interlude for a few years, but his/her "home" congregation continues to provide the proving ground for continuing development and lifelong service. Hence, a focus on church-based or home-grown leadership development is crucial. What happens in the local church precedes, compliments, supplements and legitimizes what happens in Christian higher education.

The vast majority of Christian leaders never participate in Christian higher education. Their only place for selection or development is in a local congregation. Home grown leadership development then is not only a present trend, but a normal expected pattern in the Church.

CHAPTER ONE

OVERVIEW

> *James Lambert serves as the pastor of a medium sized church. He is seeking to develop the range and numbers of leaders who will be willing and able to plant a new congregation. As he met with Paulo Cervantes, one of his key lay leaders, he wondered aloud about several questions: What kinds of leaders are needed? How many leaders of each kind are needed? Given our limited resources, how can we afford their training? If we look outside of our church, can we find men and women who will fit into our ways of doing things? If we engage in a leadership development program, should we do it?*

Informed local church leaders are interested in developing other Christian leaders. Some of us see ourselves as leaders being developed, some of us see ourselves as leader developers and some of us more appropriately see ourselves in both ways. Whether we are engaged in the equipping of others or are being equipped as Christian leaders the church is both the developmental context and the arena for exercising one's influence.

Chapter Previews

I intend to stimulate your thinking more clearly about spiritual leadership and spiritual leadership development. The first chapter provides an overview to the whole leadership development process.

To lay a base in the second chapter, "Understanding Leadership," some common leadership myths are exposed. A more wholistic Christian perspective of leadership then replaces these myths.

Chapter three, "Identifying Biblical Leadership Values," treats the issue of biblical values for Christian leaders. It seeks to answer the questions of "How can we evaluate Christian leadership?" and "Are there standards by which Christian leaders will be judged?"

Chapter four, "Emergence Patterns for Spiritual Leaders," addresses the question of how a spiritual leader emerges. How can we study the issue? Who is involved? What are the theological bases? What patterns should we expect? This chapter seeks to provide a base for our reflecting on our own emergence as leaders and the understanding of how others may also emerge as leaders.

Chapters five, six and seven treat the issue of intentionally developing leaders. Chapter five introduces the role of the Holy Spirit in leadership development. His initiating and superintending role provides the key to effective leadership development. He guides in the whole process both with the emerging leader and the existing leaders, and in the context where they serve. While the provision of spiritual gifts is a crucial part of His work, He is much more broadly and deeply involved.

Chapter six identifies some of the key roles of existing leaders in the development of other leaders. Whatever type one is as a leader, leadership development is seen as one of the key functions. Existing leaders serve in a mediating role between the Holy Spirit and the emerging leaders, reflecting the Spirit's work and putting hands, voice and a face to express His direction. Existing leaders serve as key contextualizing participants in the process. While they may be involved in training, the formal training is seen as only one of many essential component parts in the development of spiritual leaders.

Chapter seven addresses the role of the emerging leader. What must she do? What must he do? How does the role of the emergent leader mesh with the roles of the Holy Spirit and other leaders? The development of other leaders certainly is not the only thing a leader must do, but it may well be the most important leadership function. Through the development of other leaders one can expect significant personal development as well. In giving attention to the development of others, every relevant leadership issue for one's own context and for the learners' context will likely come into focus, including such diverse issues as values and organizational culture on the one hand to the existing leaders' relationships with their superiors and peers on the other. Issues of skills, knowledge and attitudes will come into focus along with the employment of power and transitions.

Basic Perspectives

Leadership development provides one window to look at current leadership and the next generation of leaders. It also provides a practical way both to recognize the complexities of leadership while at the same time addressing practical leadership issues in one's area of responsibility. This book seeks to identify a current evangelical perspective about leadership and then address the question of how to develop Christian leaders in a local context. The local context may be in Kerela, Kansas, or Kenya. The principles and the theological values remain the same. The specific local values, leadership forms and development methods, however, will differ with each local context. Leadership development as seen in this book includes training, but is also concerned with the context, followers of the emerging leader and the longer-term ongoing emergence of the person as a maturing Christian.

The view of leadership taken in this book emerges from basic biblical images such as servant, shepherd and steward. Leadership is seen as a complex process of influence in which leaders and followers interact in a context or a series of contexts over time. The effectiveness of the leadership process is contingent on a wide variety of contextual variables, some of which are influenced by the leader(s) and followers and some over which they have no influence.

To provide a base for the development of Christian leaders a broader understanding of leadership, however, is needed. The following chapter begins to address this issue of understanding leadership in the context of not only the church, but the secular communities in which we live.

CHAPTER TWO

UNDERSTANDING LEADERSHIP

As Pastor James Lambert and Paulo Cervantes continued to discuss the possibility of designing a leadership development program, Paulo raised a question for Pastor James. "If leaders are born, how will we know who to select for our training? Or, is training really needed? Maybe leaders are people who just rise to meet the need."

Pastor James asked, "Would not the traits list you use in your business along with the lists in 1 Timothy and Titus better serve to guide us in our selection and training?"

Paulo responded, "But, the church situation is different from my business. I am not sure it would work. Would not the differences in the purpose, organizational structure and primary set of activities lead in different directions?"

We live in a complex world which demands increasingly competent leaders whose ministries exemplify biblical ideals in culturally appropriate forms and methods.

An understanding of leaders and how they lead serves to undergird an approach to their development. The way we look at leadership should enable us to 1) explain the complexity of the internal and external influences in the situation; 2) predict what is likely to happen in a period of accelerated change; and, 3) pro-

9

vide a coherent, understandable and comprehensive basis for action which gives some assurance of effectiveness.

The way we look at leadership must account for the cultural values, forms and meanings of the leader and the led, and the revealed and authoritative values given to us by God in the Scriptures. Our leadership perspective then should allow us to 1) understand what is, 2) to predict what is likely to occur, and 3) to act.

An understanding of leadership can help us both to lead better and to equip others as leaders. The purpose of this chapter is to understand a basic leadership perspective so that we can explain what is happening and chart our ways to better influence our followers and develop them as leaders.

Common Leadership Problems

Many leadership problems currently militate against both clear thinking and effective leadership among our churches. *Growth* is placing unmet demands on leaders in some areas. *Non-growth* is frustrating leaders and discouraging churches in some areas. *Over-functioning leaders* (those who try to do everything and decide everything) are discouraging the development of Christian leaders in many churches. *Non-functioning leaders* are allowing churches to die. *Under-developed leaders* are not leading to their potentials in many churches. *Over-trained leaders* are discouraged and discouraging some churches. *Inappropriately trained leaders* continue to do all of the "right things" in the wrong places, at the wrong times and in the wrong ways. *Inappropriately selected leaders* aspire to leadership and misuse power. *Drop-out leaders* continue to fill the ranks of government and private business.[1]

Churches face leadership issues regardless of their size, age, culture, composition, socio-economic status, or denominational affiliation. Typical church problems include resources, conflict, decline, lack of commitment, decline in spirituality, overworked pastors, growth, and inadequate facilities.

Churches also face a number of problems because of the ways they approach leadership and leadership development. Churches are often overly influenced by secular leadership models. The theories used to explain leadership and to provide bases for action are frequently outmoded and inadequate. Occasionally, the means available for influence are misused. Christian leaders often lack an understanding of spiritual power and of their potential spiritual authority. The selection and development processes churches use occasionally malfunction with the result that many people in the churches passively sit back to watch leaders lead. Leadership values in the church generally reflect local cultural values and frequently conflict with biblical values.

Inappropriate Cultural Models

Leadership is nearly always closely tied to local cultural models. With this close association the Christian distinctives are often compromised. For example, in the U.S. the American Management Association's perspective on management serves the business community well, but often does not fit or serve the church well. We often mistakenly equate management with leadership. We take the management models well-designed for capitalistic profit-making organizations and apply them both in terms of organization and leadership to the church. This application often goes outside the range of the permissible church polity revealed in scripture. Churches frequently incorporate the local pattern of the political system into their structures and then insist it is the "Christian system." Unintentionally and too often naively we institute inappropriate and disruptive leadership models as well. However, no single people has a monopoly on this trend. In Latin America the patron/caudillo leadership models trouble many churches. Among many African peoples the Egalitarian rule of the old men or Chieftain models restrict the churches' potentials for evangelism, church planting and nurture. The American democratic model is no more appropriate. Inappropriate cultural leadership models often trouble the church.

Inadequate Leadership Perspectives

In the West five major theoretical perspectives have served over the past 150 years to explain leadership and provide a base for leading. Each approach presents some strengths and some glaring weaknesses. Each succeeding set of theories has sought to compensate for the weaknesses of the preceding perspective while adding the principal concerns of the era in which it was conceived.

Unfortunately, some Christian leaders are still looking through the one-hundred-fifty-year-old antiquated leadership perspectives and wondering why the secular world, non-Christian religions and syncretistic cults are seriously challenging us in influencing the peoples around us.

Enough truth or validity remains in each of these perspectives to stir our acceptance of their credibility. However, we often fail to acknowledge their weaknesses or to note the historical and cultural contexts from which they emerged.

While space does not allow, similar examples could be cited from the images of the Indian guru, the African chief, the Hispanic caudillo or patron, church leadership is still explained and implemented around these theories.

Great Man Theories

The first of these sets of theories is popularly known as the Great Man Theories.[2] Two basic perspectives occur in and persist from this set of theories: 1) Leaders are born; and 2) leaders simply emerge due to the social pressures of the situation. Much evidence has been suggested to support these theories. Many kings and other national leaders have come from families where leadership seemed to be inherited. Look at the Nehrus, Kennedys or the Rockefellers. Look at the Hapsburgs or the Tudors. Look at the extended dynasties in ancient Egypt and China.

The social side of these theories also musters evidence for its support. Some would point to Winston Churchill, Abraham Lincoln, George Washington, Mao Tse Tung, Golda Meir, Martin Luther King, Lech Walensa and many other world-known leaders and show how the times and situations in which they lived demanded strong leaders. Therefore, their societal situations simply made leaders of these people who otherwise would have remained unknown followers.

Many Christian leaders still debate whether leaders are born or made. Leaders are both born and made. The potential for leadership is a God-given capacity which may—or may not—be developed. And, one can certainly point to the situation to see the environmental effects on the development of a leader. However, this set of theories provides no reliable way either to select leaders or to equip them for service. These theories only seek (and that inadequately) to explain how leaders emerge.

Trait Theories

Moving into the "scientific era," researchers began to see the weaknesses of the Great Man approach to leadership. Nineteen hundred and four was the date of a shift toward a new paradigm whose influence also remains with us even today.[3] The Trait Theories suggested that by identifying leaders' traits one could both select effective leaders and train people to be effective leaders.

Several related assumptions are still widely held: 1) Persons who consistently lead effectively will possess certain traits. 2) Empirical research should be able to relate leader traits to effectiveness. 3) Predictions about who will be effective leaders can be done by utilizing measures which identify the traits in empirical research. 4) Leadership training would be helpful for only those people with the inherent leadership traits.[4]

Early research seemed to support the validity of this approach because nearly all of the research was done in the same kind of situation—factories. However, as the leadership studies ranged further afield, thousands of leadership traits were identified.[5] Their usefulness in predicting leadership effectiveness proved ineffective. The training of people to have particular traits or characteristics did not result in significantly-improved leadership effectiveness. Ralph Stogdill of the Ohio State University Center for Leadership Studies published his perspective-shifting article in 1948 in which he, through careful documentation, demonstrated the weaknesses of this approach to understanding leadership. He showed that there are no consistent traits which predict effective leadership.

Peter Drucker simply asserts,

> ... charisma does not by itself guarantee effectiveness as a leader ... Nor are there any such things as 'leadership qualities' or a 'leadership personality.' Franklin D. Roosevelt, Winston Churchill, George Marshall, Dwight Eisenhower, Bernard Montgomery and Douglas MacArthur, were all highly effective—and highly visible—leaders during World War II. No two of them shared any 'personality traits' or any qualities.[6]

Before 1948, universal traits of leadership were emphasized. After that, specific situational assessments took over, in fact dominated the field, much more than argued for by Stogdill.[7] Both individual traits and situational assessments as well as the interaction between them are important, and that was Stogdill's main thesis.[8]

When one is involved in the process of selection, traits still inevitably come into focus. However, now traits are considered much more in terms of the context where the leader is to serve. As these traits are considered along with other leadership variables such as the followers, the situation and shared values also come into focus.

Behavioral Theories

The next and more contemporaneous set of leadership studies focused on leader behavior. These studies brought two different kinds of leader behavior into focus: a task orientation and a relationship orientation. After Stogdill's 1948 landmark article,[9] many people at several universities began to study leadership behavior. After several hundred studies in the U.S., American writers generally agreed that two independent kinds of leader behavior served to explain what leaders do. Stogdill described these behaviors as "consideration" and the "initiation of structure."[10] Others commonly described them as "relational" and "task" behaviors.

However, these behavior-based theories had serious limits as well. While the behavior of the leader was increasingly related to the desired behavior of the follower, the interaction of the situation still was not clearly brought into focus. In these theories the issues of the values of the leaders were considered, but the values of the community or followers were not generally regarded. Furthermore, the interactions of the leader, follower(s) and situation were not all brought together into a coherent explanation.

These perspectives by themselves do not serve well to predict leadership effectiveness because they do not bring the influences of the leadership situation into focus. When applied cross-culturally these two categories of leader behavior often do not match local leadership categories. Yet, many Christian writers still seek to describe as a major focus of their work an appropriate balance between a task orientation and a relational orientation for leaders.

When considering leadership, however, and leadership styles, leader behavior must always be brought into focus. Leadership styles are most simply patterned leader behavior. While the categories shift across worldview boundaries, issues of initiating structure and showing consideration remain as critical leadership issues.

Contingency Theories

Researchers recognizing that in effective leadership a contingent set of relationships exists among the leader(s), follower(s) and the situation have developed another perspective. The Contingency Paradigm of leadership suggests that leadership effectiveness is contingent not only on the leaders' behavior, but on the followers and situation as well. The contingency theories developed along two lines: 1) the "single" style theories and, 2) the multiple or flexible style theories.[11]

Only a few Christian writers have moved ahead to consider the benefits of this perspective. Helen Doohan in *Leadership in Paul* shows how Paul adjusted his leadership style to match the maturity of the churches he helped establish. She and the secular writers who treat various aspects of this model provide much useful insight into both predicting effective leadership and preparing for effective leadership.

This leadership perspective, however, presents some problems because it does not take into consideration the situation beyond the immediate followers. The leadership effectiveness in the local situation will be conditioned by the broader context. It will be conditioned by the historical precedents. It will be conditioned by the surrounding culture. It will be affected by the current political, cultural, economic, sociological, and religious context. When one crosses even subcultural boundaries, the complexities of worldview differences immediately demand attention.

Great Man, Trait, Behavioral and Simple Contingency theories, while having some validity, have all contributed to our as yet inadequate understanding of leadership. None of these theories has treated the unique issues which arise in "Christian leadership" nor the complexities which arise in inter-cultural or cross-cultural leadership situations.

Complex Contingency Theories

Recognizing the validity of the contingency theories, Yukl[12] and others have begun to introduce more complexity into the contingency theories. Within this perspective the local leadership context is considered as well as the broader context with all of its complexities. Unfortunately, many Christian leaders have not recognized the complexities of leadership.

Contemporary secular writers[13] recognize the complexities of leadership. They suggest that no pre-planned approach will suffice, but that the only way through the maze is by a strong commitment to a set of values. Integrity is the key in the diverse possibilities of alternatives of behaviors and leadership styles. Integrity provides stability along the slippery road of relativism, politics and the risks of leadership.

The complexities of effective leadership require some strong means to bring focus to the whole process. The key to bringing this focus is one's value base. Joseph Badaracco and Richard Ellsworth write in *Leadership and the Quest for Integrity* of the central role of values.[14]

These complexities of leadership are best met by leaders who with a strong sense of values, seek to transform both the followers and the broader context. J. M. Burns describes this "transformational leadership" as a way "leaders and followers raise one another to higher levels of morality and motivation." [15] Leaders effectively change the followers and the situation by making them aware of the values of the outcomes, building values around the group-organization or team, and by raising the standard of their motivation.

This book is written in the light of theories. However, because these theories tend to be very Western in perspective,. they also tend to focus on issues in the business community and so often have a production or marketing bias.

Metaphor-Based Theories

The complexities of leadership are not unknown in non-Western or traditional societies. In fact, the ways of treating these complexities in non-Western societies serve as enriching complements or supplements to the Western student of leadership.

The complexities may be seen in the rich variety of metaphors used to describe leaders and leadership. The imagery of the metaphor serves both to expand the concepts of leadership on the one hand and to delimit other metaphors on the other. For example, three biblical metaphors used in this text serve to show both the complexity and integration of a biblical view of leadership.

The use of each metaphor reflects cultural values, delimitations of status and role, and implications related to the use of power. Since both status and roles come in "sets," the expectations of both leader and followers in a given situation are implicit in the metaphor. Hence a steward or trustee had a special kind of relationship with the owner or trustor and a culturally-expected role to play with the trust.

The use of a multiplicity of metaphors allows one to see the shape of the whole even as one can only see the shape of a finely cut diamond by viewing many facets. Not all the metaphors will be as large as the others, but each one is important. Jesus used about thirty-five metaphors in the gospels to describe the construct of followership. His teachings about followership are critically important to understand the idea of leadership in the epistles.

This text then will also draw on this metaphorical approach to explain some ideas about leadership and leadership development.

Misuse of Influence Means

Another set of problems facing the church and Christian leaders is the misuse of influence. Leaders may have a variety of influence means available through several different kinds of power, the structure(s) of the organization or community of which they are a part, and their status (both ascribed and achieved). Without the solid application of Christian values or ethics, any of these influence means available to the Christian leader may be misused.

In addition to spiritual power which comes from the Holy Spirit's working in one's life, several other kinds of power may be used. Paul Hersey and Kenneth Blanchard define power as "influence potential."[16] Dennis Wrong describes power as "the intended, successful control of others."[17] Machiavelli suggested that there are two basic power sources: fear and love. In modern literature fear is related to position power and love is related to personal power. A third and for Christians a primary kind of power is spiritual power. Hersey and Blanchard describe seven kinds of power.[18] Each one may be available to Christian leaders in addition to spiritual power. However, each one must be used only within revealed value constraints.

We can reflect about any one kind of power and identify Christian leaders who have abused it. The results of the misuse of power are seen in church decline, splits, spiritual barrenness, ineffectiveness, jealousy, envy, factions and strife.

Other inappropriate "tactics" or uses of "illegitimate" influence means also occur in the church or parachurch contexts. Ted Ward suggests that manipulative tactics are too often used in the church. He suggests that these tactics are seen in a leadership style characterized by the controlling of others to one's own advantage through playing on guilt, fear, divisions, gossip or other such means. This problem relates to the recent concern for the development of management skills drawn from secular management. Leaders often lack awareness of the possible range of approaches to people and therefore they resort to tactics that are imprudent and, in the final analysis, childish.[19]

The primary task of the church and of "spiritual" leaders is "spiritual." It requires spiritual power to "wrestle" not with people but as the apostle Paul writes,

> For we are not fighting against people made of flesh and blood, but against persons without bodies—the evil rulers of the unseen world, those mighty satanic beings and great evil princes of darkness who rule this world; and against huge numbers of wicked spirits in the spirit world. [Ephesians 6:12]

The misuse of or lack of use of spiritual power may well be one of the most serious problems facing Christian leaders in any culture.

The misuse of influence means then continues to be a serious leadership problem among the churches. This issue requires resolution in many situations before any other progress in either leadership development or leadership effectiveness can be made.

Inappropriate Selection Processes

Inappropriate selection processes may occur in any culture. Indians following the traditional guru model may wait twelve years before appointing a person to a position of leadership. Americans like democratic processes and are proud of being a "democratic" nation. They boast of their political heritage which holds as an ideal that their government is of the people, by the people and for the people. However, American democratic political processes provide many dysfunctional pitfalls for Christian leadership processes, not the least of which is the selection of leaders. This democratic process often succeeds in the churches in the selection of the most popular or most politically powerful with only a rhetorical concern for the most qualified.

Some churches select local leaders on the basis of relational ties. Most people would criticize that approach because little guarantee exists that the person either will be accepted as a leader, will be qualified or will be committed to lead.

People who move ahead to consider qualifications often base their choice on academic qualifications. By looking solely at academic qualifications a search committee can be assured of a person's ability to succeed in school, but not in his/her ability to succeed in leading. One can generally be assured of the person's valuing an "intellectual meritocracy" because of the value employed in the selection. However, we can not be assured that the person will value ministry or be an effective leader.

Others seek an approach and look at a person's traits—his/her character, his/her size, intelligence, capacity to lead, achievement, responsibility, status, cooperativeness, humor, and/or other traits which should guarantee an effective leader. However, too often disappointment prevails because the leader does not do well in the new situation because the traits are not appropriate. Or, the leader uses a leadership style which is appropriate in business, but not in the church.

Our leadership selection processes closely follow the dominant patterns in our culture as do the selection processes in other cultures. That may be why some of our "Christian" leaders look and act like leaders in other social organizations in our societies but fail in the issues of ministry and spirituality.

Passivity of the "Laity"

Many churches suffer from a general passivity of the people of God. In these churches often nearly all of the leadership functioning is delegated to the paid staff. The paid staff members are expected to be "multi-gifted" and are "hired" with that kind of set of qualifications in mind. Such a problem greatly inhibits every form of growth in the church and often blocks the multiplication of new churches.

The following quotation comes from a church policy manual which the senior pastoral and administrative staff of a church with about a thousand members presented to the elders of that congregation for ratification in late 1991.[20] As of the time of this writing, this church has serious financial problems, a sense of frustration because of the lack of "lay leaders" and little commitment among its adult members to either evangelize the communities it serves or to "disciple all the nations."

> The purposes of (name of the church) are achieved and accomplished through the employment of competent and committed staff. It is recognized that employees are best able to fulfill their responsibilities when work assignments, expectations and conditions are as clearly stated as possible and are conducive to the achievements of both quality and quantity job performance.

These limited and inappropriate leadership perspectives push sensitive Christian leaders to consider more biblical and cultural approaches to understand leadership.

Toward a More Appropriate View of Leadership

With these seemingly overwhelming problems and these influential, but flawed leadership perspectives, how should we then view Christian leadership? Three basic biblical concepts will serve to focus the development of a Christian perspective of leadership. These primary concepts describe leaders as servants, shepherds and stewards. From these basic concepts emerge definitions to serve the Christian community.

Leadership Defined

Most simply defined, **leadership is the process of influence.** The process always includes a number of key components: leaders, followers, a situation in which they interact; means for influence which emerge from the leader and from the community; values; time for the interactions to occur; and goals which the leader(s) and followers seek to achieve. Leadership is a complex influence process in which leaders and followers interact in a context or a series of contexts over time. Within this context the leaders exercise influence with the followers toward a mutually desired goal. The effectiveness of the leadership process is contingent on a wide variety of contextual variables, some of which are influenced by the leader(s) and followers and some over which they have no influence.

J. R. Clinton offers a useful contemporary definition which reflects a "complex contingency"[21] leadership perspective:

Leadership is
1) a dynamic process over an extended period of time,
2) in various situations in which a leader utilizing leadership resources,
3) and by specific leadership behaviors,
4) influences the thoughts and activity of followers,
5) toward accomplishment of person/task aims,
6) mutually beneficent for leaders, followers and the macro context of which they are a part.[22]

In addition to these six important components in Clinton's definition, two important issues must be added. The worldview of the leader, followers and the community in which they live must also be considered. Within this worldview one can find what is commonly described as philosophy, and values. One's theology also flows out of his/her worldview. A second consideration is the interactional dynamics of the variables. One can not separate the influence of the leader, followers and situation from values and influence means. All are inextricably interwoven in a dynamic influence process.

Christian leadership, however, differs from secular, business, or political leadership. Ward captures this difference by asserting that leadership models for the church "must be drawn from the scripture and evaluated in terms of accountability to Christ."[23] These leadership models move away from the focus of personal and corporate power which aim at personal advantage so typical of non-Christian settings. These models focus on spiritual power and authority as the primary influence means of achieving God's purpose.

Clinton captures this distinctive by describing a Christian leader as:

> A person with God-given capacity and God-given responsibility to influence a specific group of God's people toward God's purposes for the group.[24]

As Christian leaders we need to understand what spiritual leadership is and how it functions both to improve our own leading and to better equip others as they lead. God has called us not only to do the work of ministry, but to multiply others who will serve and equip others also.

Definitions from a Western deductive and linear way of thinking are absent in the Scriptures and foreign to much of the present non-Western world. The absence of propositional definitions does not mean, however, that the complexities of leadership are not appreciated or understood. Rather, these complexities are treated with complex imagery which allows local contextual application and expansion. Multiple metaphors are like the facets of a finely cut jewel. Each reflects a face with its distinctive hues, but is defined by other metaphors which reflect other hues. Only when taken together is the whole understood. Through the whole of the Scriptures scores of metaphors and other figures of speech are used to describe leaders and followers. Three key biblical metaphors reveal the larger facets of a Christian leadership perspective. They include servant, shepherd and steward. These three metaphors have different cultural referents today and so require close exegetical attention to see clearly their original brilliance and subtle hues, and to know how to apply them in today's situations.

Leader as Servant

The spiritual leader is one who voluntarily or willingly submits to the sovereign authority (lordship) of Jesus Christ to obey Him as directed for His benefit. The leader's capacity (giftedness), role, status, placement, and tenure are all under the sovereign authority of Jesus Christ and overseen by the Holy Spirit. The benefits of the serving are for His pleasure which results in the good of the church and the ultimate good of the servant. However, along the way the servant may experience harassment, inconvenience and various kinds of testing. The agenda is the Lord's, not the servant's, nor that of the other believers who may also benefit from the service. Lawrence Richards notes the key and *critical* concept underlying Christian leadership and ministry as "one of service and support of others.[25]

Leader as Shepherd

A second primary concept which provides an understanding of Christian leadership is that of "shepherd." Spiritual leaders are called and commissioned to function as shepherds. As shepherds they are to tend the flock of God. This tending includes a variety of functions which follow the analogy of shepherding such as feeding (teaching), nurturing (exhorting, reproving, correcting, comforting), protecting, congregating (maintaining group cohesion), leading or guiding, calling to follow, knowing by name, modeling and leading in hope. Shepherds are not only called and commissioned to function in these positive ways, they are warned about taking advantage of the flock for personal gain, lording it over the flock, leading for money and being careless (cf. 1 Pet 5:1–5).

Leader as Steward

A third undergirding concept for Christian leadership is "stewardship." Spiritual leaders are entrusted with the message of the gospel, gifts for ministry, and a missiological task or ministry to perform. The commission is seen in terms of a "trust" or a "stewardship." The leader is seen then as a trustee. Trustees are expected to guard what has been entrusted to them (1 Ti 6:20). They are expected to employ the trust to the owner's advantage and according to His will. The functioning of Christian leaders ought to be seen in terms of obediently serving, shepherding and stewarding as directed by what God has revealed.

It should be noted that none of these three images of leaders suggest a high status or high degree of personal or corporate power.

Cultural Variables in Leadership

Different contexts will require somewhat different specific descriptions of different kinds of leaders. Differences in the context may also make a difference in terms of the number of the "types" of Christian leaders. Some of the variables which will affect the ways these leader types will be defined include the age, size and polity of the church, and the culture(s) in which the church functions (broader culture and specific "corporate" culture).

Geerte Hofstede suggests four sets of variables which affect leadership configurations: 1) Power Distance, 2) Uncertainty Avoidance, 3) Individualism-Collectivism, and 4) Masculinity-Femininity.[26] Power Distance is "the extent to which a society accepts the fact that power in institutions and organizations is distributed unequally."[27] Uncertainty Avoidance is "the extent to which a society feels threatened by uncertain and ambiguous situations and tries to avoid these situations by providing greater career stability, establishing more formal rules, not tolerating deviant ideas and behaviors, and believing in absolute truths and the attainment of expertise."[28] Individualism "implies a loosely knit social framework in which people are supposed to take care of themselves and their immediate families."[29] Collectivism is "characterized by a tight social framework in which people distinguish between in-groups and out-groups; they expect their in-group (relatives, clan, organizations) to look after them, and in exchange for that they feel they owe absolute loyalty to it."[30] Hofstede describes "Masculinity" as a cultural characteristic as "assertiveness, the acquisition of money and things, and not caring for others, the quality of life, or people."[31] On the other hand, he describes "feminine" cultures as the direct opposite of these "masculine" characteristics. The combination of these configurations deeply affect how leaders are distributed (i.e., both the numbers of leaders in each type and the number of types), the perceived distance between the types of leaders, as well as the status and role sets of each type of leader.

Some of the specific variables within each type are "generic" and will apply differently in different church contexts. For example, expectations about the issues of training, levels of pro-

fessionalization, and being salaried or not will vary somewhat
from church to church in different subcultural contexts.

Types of Leaders

Christian leaders may be classified into five general types.[32]
These five kinds of leaders differ in terms of the nature of their
ministries (whether direct or indirect), sphere of influence, use
of influence or power, roles, status, type and amount of related
training, degree of professionalization and distribution. They
also differ significantly in terms of kinds of experience they
have. They are not, however, distributed on a value scale. All
are highly valued and considered essential before the Lord and in
the church (cf. 1 Co 12). Figures One and Two show the essential distinctions of these five kinds of leaders.[33]

Another variable which ought to be seen through each of the
five types of leaders is spiritual/ministry maturity. While one
may be spiritually mature as a Type I leader and have a mature
ministry, other types of leaders emerge from this base. One may
be called to be another kind of leader and progress through the
various types of leadership en route to maturity in ministry. One
should not assume that a Type I or II leader is immature spiritually or immature in terms of ministry development. However,
one would expect that as one emerges as a Type IV or Type V
leader that there would be on the average a greater degree of
maturity. One would expect a convergence of giftedness, status
and role in one's ministry.

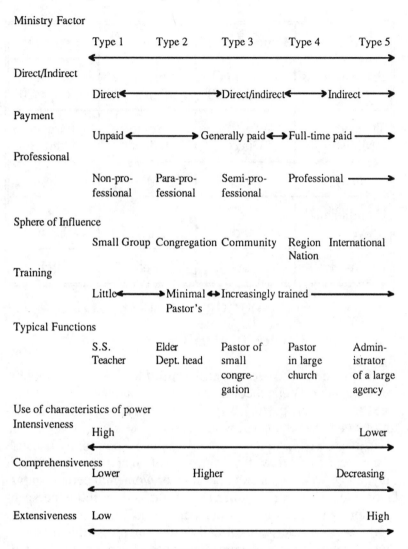

FIGURE ONE

Contrastive Continuum of Types of Leaders

Variable	Types I & II	Type III	Type IV
Extensiveness	Cell, small group, < 20	small congregation, < 200	large congregation, > 200
Type of Ministry	Direct	Some Indirect	Largely indirect
Intensity	High	Mid	Low
Comprehensiveness	Mid	High	Low
Extensiveness	Low	Mid	High

FIGURE TWO

Leader Distinctives by Type

The leaders who serve in each type of leadership are not limited by gender. While theological debates continue about specific roles (e.g., elder, pastor), I find no biblical justification to distinguish between men and women on the basis of giftedness, the basis of leadership in the church. In a given community because of the local worldview, theological position and church polity, it may not be wise to install either men or women in certain statuses or roles. However, neither in terms of a descriptive perspective nor from a theological perspective do I find any reason to assign or to restrict categorically either men or women from a given type of leadership simply because of gender. Traditionally, women have been more or less limited to Types I and II whereas all five types have been open to men.

While age is not a primary variable in understanding leadership, it does play a role. The spiritual and social maturity that is required for each type of leadership emerges out of life experience. Generally, more is required as an entry level for each "successive" type of leader. However, one should not assume that as one becomes older one automatically moves from one type of leader to another. One can point to exceptions, but men and women who would be Types IV and V are generally more than thirty-five years old, whereas entry into Types I and II may come as early as the teens or twenties. Cultural constraints play an important part regarding age as well.

Type I

Type I leaders voluntarily serve without pay in a local, limited sphere of influence. They minister directly or face-to-face. They relate to their ministry as non-professionals. These roles generally do not require specialized or formal training. While not needing a high level of training, these roles remain the most numerous leadership roles in the church. Typical on-professional roles include small group leader, Sunday School teacher, choir director, organist, youth sponsor. In non-Western churches catechists often fit into this category. Then extensiveness or extensive number of people influenced by a Type I leader is limited to a small number, often between one and ten. The comprehensiveness of their influence or range of lifestyle issues is limited. However, the intensity or degree of their influence is potentially high.

This type of leader is critically important to the health and growth of a church. New believers have most of their contact with these leaders and new believers work in these first ministries and leadership development situations with Type I leaders. Type I leaders carry the primary responsibilities for shepherding and instructing the majority of the members of the church through small groups in the church.

Type II

Type II leaders voluntarily serve in a local, church-wide sphere of influence. Their ministry is direct or face-to-face. They are typically paraprofessionals, that is, they work alongside professionals with either mature experience or some specialized training. Elders or deacons in a local congregation would generally fit into this category. The extent of their influence reaches beyond their immediate associates to many related small groups.

A department superintendent who oversees small groups or Sunday School classes would be a Type II leader. In non-Western settings the unpaid evangelist who works in the local or surrounding communities would be a Type II leader. The comprehensiveness of their influence is potentially greater than the Type I leader. And the intensity or degree of their influence around a single issue is potentially high.

Paraprofessional leaders serve alongside or in the place of professionals. Paraprofessionals are seen in several professions—paramedics and paralegals have had specific, but limited training. In growing churches in the Two-Thirds World this kind of leader often carries the heaviest burden of leadership. Often the church can not afford higher-level training or the salaries sometimes expected by the higher-trained leaders. In a church situation paraprofessionals may or may not be employed. Often they are not employed. An example of a paraprofessional is a trained "lay counselor" who serves alongside the professional on a part-time basis and who would refer cases too difficult on to the professional. Itinerant evangelists and catechists fit into this category in many Two-Thirds World countries.

Type III

Type III leaders are generally paid and working full time in western churches. Many Type III leaders in the Two-Thirds World are bivocational. Pastors of small congregations would typically be in this category. They have a local community sphere of influence. Their primary sphere of influence is direct, but they have some indirect ministry. They would be considered as semiprofessional because they would typically have met the minimal entry requirements, such as a basic theological education, spiritual maturity, and ministry experience, to enter a paid "pastoral" role. Generally, they are eligible for ordination or moving toward ordination. The extensiveness of their influence would reach into the local community beyond the local church. The comprehensiveness of their influence is generally wide among the people in their sphere of influence. The intensity of their influence is potentially high.

Type IV

Type IV leaders are typically pastors of a multi-staff or at least a multiple-cell congregation[34] or administrators of small agencies. They generally have a regional sphere of influence in other congregations or agencies. Their influence is mostly indirect. Type IV leaders are considered professionals, having completed their training and demonstrated both their competence and commitment. The extensiveness of their influence reaches beyond the people with whom they have direct contact. The comprehensiveness of their influence is probably at its peak. The intensity of their influence, while great in a specific area, may be much less in other areas. A "circuit-riding" pastor who serves several congregations should be considered a Type IV leader.

Type V

Type V leaders serve in national or international leadership roles. Their ministry is indirect beyond a second level. They are also considered professionals. The extensiveness or reach of their influence is greater than other types of leader in terms of the numbers of people influenced. The comprehensiveness of their influence is generally less with their increasing specialty. The intensity of their influence is high with only a few individuals and in limited areas of influence and tends to decrease toward the outer reaches of their sphere of influence.

Leaders who influence indirectly across national or international regions through denominational structures, writing, and teaching in theological education would fit as Type V leaders. Their influence is indirect. They only know the "kinds" of people their leadership is intended to influence.

If one charts the distribution of the five kinds of leaders on the basis of the number of people to whom a person can effectively relate and effectively influence, an interesting distribution pattern emerges. For the sake of simplicity and to suggest some guidelines, the following table presents one such approach. (See Table Two.) One basic assumption is that a given person has a limited potential for direct, regular, face-to-face influence. The number of people one may regularly directly influence at a worldview level may range between ten and twenty. Another assumption is that a set of five levels of leaders appears to be adequate to describe types of leadership in both the church and parachurch structures.[35]

This distribution, while imperfect, does suggest the relative numbers of each kind of worker. The sheer numbers of people involved in Types I and II should capture our attention. David Rambo[36] while only treating Types IV and V, supports the need for the limited number of these kinds of leaders.

TABLE ONE

Relative Distribution of Leader Types for a Community of 100,000[37]

Number of Leaders Required:	Leaders who relate face to face with			
	5 people	10 people	15 people	20 people
Type I	20,000	10,000	6,667	5,000
Type II	4,000	1,000	444	250
Type III	160	100	30	13
Type IV	32	10	2	1
Type V	6	1	0	0

If the theory is valid, each type of leader must be equipped. However, special attention should be given to Types I and II because of their potential for overall impact. Type III should not be neglected because of their potential for multiplying Types I and II. Types IV and V should receive attention because of the potential numbers of people who may be influenced and because of their more comprehensive view which aids in strategic planning.

TABLE TWO

Potential for Influence on Individuals
for Types of Leaders

Leader type	Extensiveness	Comprehensiveness	Intensity	Total Potential for Influence
Type I	1	5	5	11
Type II	2	4	4	10
Type III	3	3	3	9
Type IV	4	2	2	8
Type V	5	1	1	7

The vast majority of church workers needed are in Types I, II, and III. These people generally have the lowest entry-level skills and knowledge, may need more encouragement and instruction, are culturally or socially within the context which is the focus of the development, and have the least accessibility to/from formal educational institutions (geographically, politically, economically, academically and/or socially). They lack the resources for training and are the least visible.

By "extracting" people from Types I and II to "change" or "develop" them toward Types III, IV or V several dysfunctional results may emerge: 1) Too many may be trained for those existing status/role positions. 2) The potential for local influence decreases. 3) A greater passivity often emerges locally along with a greater level of dependency. 4) The most able local leaders are "drained" from the local leadership increasing the difficulty for the Types III, IV, and V leaders to influence locally. 5) The cost/benefit ratio investment of our training programs may continue to be skewed in favor of the higher-trained people.

Churches have often reversed the priority of assigning training resources with the distribution of these five kinds of leaders. The greater resources are assigned to the few (Types IV and V), whereas little is allocated to the development of Types I and II who may outnumber Types IV and V by several hundred times.

For basic planning, leaders should be developed at no smaller ratio than shown in the following chart:

Type I   1 for every 5–10

Type II   1 for every 25–50

Type III   1 for every 100–200

Type IV   1 for every 200–1000

Type V   1 for every 1000–10,000

While a church or agency will likely be able to function effectively with less leaders, the above table allows for growth within the ministry of each of these leaders as they are emerging.

Table Three summarizes the distinctives for each kind of leader in terms of a set of basic curricular issues would be contrastively applied to each kind of leader. The developmental/curricular approach typically shifts from informal (unplanned, unstructured) to nonformal (planned, short cycle, function oriented) to formal (planned, long cycle, theoretical) to nonformal types of education as one seeks to equip types one through five leaders.

Local church-based leadership development typically includes both informal and nonformal components. Many smaller churches establish relationships with formal institutions (Bible institutes, Bible colleges, seminaries, or Christian universities) as partners to develop the full range of leaders in a full range of equipping opportunities.

TABLE THREE

Development Distinctives for Each Type of Leader

Curricular Issues	Type I & II	Type III	Type IV	Type V
Purpose	Small group leadership	Small congregation leadership	Large congregation leadership or small Christian agency leadership	National International leadership in administration, teaching, or writing
Content	Specific skills and limited knowledge	Generalizable skills and knowledge management skills	Knowledge of theories and theory application	Knowledge theories and theory construction
Timing	Short cycle, at the convenience of the learner	Long cycle, at the convenience of the institution	Short cycle, at the convenience of the learner	Short cycle, at the convenience of the learner
Resources	Limited amount needed, usually available from the learner and the community being served	Resource intensive, many resources needed, often outside subsidies are needed	Moderate resources needed	Low to moderate resources needed
Costs	Minimal	High	Moderate	Low
Delivery System	Informal, modeling, apprenticeships	Formal, highly structured	More nonformal, less structured	Informal, mentoring, apprenticed
Control	Partially external to the learner	Largely external to the learner	Increasingly self-selected	Self-selected or by agency served
Spiritual Formation	Focus on foundations and on doing	Focus moving from doing to being	Focus on converging status, role and giftedness	Focus on convergence

Leadership Functions

Leadership functions for Christian leaders should be approached initially using biblical concepts and then as one has internalized these biblical perspectives, many insights may be gleaned from the secular disciplines of management, sociology, anthropology, leadership and education. Three basic biblical leadership metaphors have already been noted, i.e., serving, shepherding and stewarding. Each of these metaphors carries an implicit set of functions. Other functions may be seen in the roles of the priest who represents the people before God and the prophet who speaks to the people for God. When one asks, "What does or should a leader do?" some contemporary Christian writers have brought some very helpful insights into the basic perspectives of serving, shepherding and stewarding. These three images are only three of at least fifty complementary images used in the New Testament of people who would learn to lead in the church. Each image reflects a facet or brings into focus a piece of the whole complex picture of Christian leadership.

The apostle Paul writes about leadership gifts in Eph. 4:13. He says that an important function or purpose of apostles, prophets, evangelists, pastors and teachers is to "equip" (train, prepare) God's people for ministry.

James Kouzes and Barry Posner suggest a complementary set of functions:

1. Challenging the process
   a. Search for opportunities
   b. Experiment and take risks
2. Inspiring a shared vision
   a. Envision the future
   b. Enlist others
3. Enabling others to act
   a. Foster collaboration
   b. Strengthen others
4. Modeling the way
   a. Set the example
   b. Plan small wins

5. Encouraging the heart
   a. Recognize contributions
   b. Celebrate accomplishments.[38]

These functions apply to each type of leader. Whether one is a Type I or a Type V leader, he/she will be involved in all of these functions from time to time. Too often leaders are narrowly or simplistically viewed in terms of only problem-solving, coordination, motivation or decision-making.

Multi-Directional Influence

Hollander's "Social Exchange" theory[39] provides a useful basis for understanding the "dynamic" or "transactional" relationship between leaders and followers. Hollander shows how each is dependent on and also benefits from the other. In addition, leaders are influenced by the situation and influence the situation. The local worldview and culture provide perspectives, patterns and values within which the leaders and followers interact. Their interactions then combine with others' experience to become a part of the shared learned experience which shapes the congregational culture and worldview.

The effective leader will over time go beyond serving in a way which allows an ongoing mutuality of influence. The effective leader will aim at transforming every key component in the leadership equation. In the short term, the followers will be brought into focus to transform their behavior, relationship, attitudes and spirituality. However, to be optimally effective a leader will seek to transform the situation where both he/she and the followers interact. Addressing issues of empowerment, removal of constraints, organizational culture development and values formation for both the followers and the leader are key transformational issues.

Transformational leaders work from a strong value base. They seek to shape or transform the leadership situation using five primary means 1) Attention. What receives the leader's attention is reshaped in response to praise, criticism, monitoring and inquiries. What is ignored followers deem unimportant. 2) Reactions to crises. How leaders respond to crises shapes the

situation. 3) Role modeling. Leaders communicate values by
what they do. Giving lip service without active support commu-
nicates a lack of value. 4) Allocation of rewards. Leaders shape
the situations and "corporate" cultures in which they serve by the
rewards they distribute related to finance, status and recognition.
5) Leaders also shape the situation by setting the criteria for
selection and dismissal.[40]

Leaders over the long term may increase their transformational impact by addressing five other organizational issues:
1) design of the organizational structure, 2) design of systems
and procedures, 3) design of facilities, 4) shaping and telling of
stories, legends and myths, and 5) formal statements.

An effective leader recognizes these interactive elements and
works within both the constraints and opportunities they afford.
The primary strategy for leading within this complexity is an
incarnational model which seeks to transform.

Summary

Leadership theorists repeatedly cite five critical issues which
require attention in the development of a leader. Often these matters are only assumed in a training process. However, since
training by itself will not produce leaders, these four concerns
demand our attention. They include the person of the leader, the
follower(s), the situation in which they interact in the leadership
process, the improvement or provision of influence means and
the values which guide and constrain the participants' behaviors.

One critical beginning point from this list of issues for every
leadership development concern is values. What are the biblical
values which undergird Christian leadership development?
Chapter three initiates some discussion around this question of
values.

End Notes

1   Adapted from Edgar J. Elliston, "Developing Christian Leaders," Address presented to the Pan-African Conference of Christian Church/ Church of Christ Missionaries, Nairobi, Kenya. July, 1985:1–2.

2   Carlyle's writings *On Heroes and Hero Worship* in 1841 led in the articulation of this perspective.

3   Bernard Bass, *Stogdill's Handbook of Leadership*. New York: The Free Press. 1981:43–96.

4   See Bass 1981:43–44.

5   See Bass 1981:43.

6   Peter F. Drucker, "Leadership: More Doing than Dash," *Wall Street Journal*, Wednesday, January 6, 1968.

7   Bernard Bass, *Stogdill's Handbook of Leadership*. New York: The Free Press. 1981:43–96.

8   See Bass 1981:43.

9   See Bass 1981:43.

10 See Bass 1981:441–392.

11 One theoretical perspective is characterized by the idea that a leader should have a single basic style. Robert Blake and Jane Mouton suggested one ideal style in their Management Grid as being high in both task and relational behaviors (Blake, R. R. and J. S. Mouton. *The Managerial Grid*. Houston: Gulf, 1964).

Fred Fiedler suggests that a leader has a limited leadership style range because of a person's personality and experience. Consequently, to be maximally effective the leader should be placed in a situation most favorable for his/her style. With the single style theorists the question of fit with the situation is crucial (Fiedler, Fred E. *A Theory of Leadership Effectiveness*. New York: McGraw Hill. 1967.)

Fiedler further holds that a leader has a dominant style which is based on his/her personality characteristics and that it is difficult to change this style. It is better then to change the situation to maximize leadership effectiveness. He also holds that consideration and the initiation of structure extend over a single continuum and are types of a leader personality. His approach, however, does not adequately consider the followers' characteristics and their response to and influence on the leader (cf. Fred E. Fiedler "The Trouble With Leadership Training Is That It Doesn't Train Leaders." In William R. Lassey and Richard R. Fernandez (eds.), *Leadership and Social Change*. La Jolla, CA: University Associates, 1976:238–246).

A second contingency perspective suggests that a leader may have multiple styles. Paul Hersey and Kenneth Blanchard suggest in their Situational Leadership Model a range over four basic styles (Telling, Selling, Participating and Delegating) which correlate with the followers' maturity (Paul Hersey and Kenneth H. Blanchard, *Management of Organizational Behavior Utilizing Human Resources* (Fifth edition) Englewood Cliffs, NJ: Prentice Hall,. 1988).

Robert House in his Path-Goal model sees the issue of leadership style as related to the task structure (Robert J. House. "A Path-Goal Theory of Leader Effectiveness," *Administrative Science Quarterly*. 1971:16: 321–338).

[12] Gary A. Yukl, *Leadership in Organizations*, Second Edition. (Englewood Cliffs, NJ: Prentice Hall, 1989).

[13] For example, Joseph L. Badaracco, Jr. and Richard R. Ellsworth, *The Quest for Integrity in Leadership* (Boston: Harvard Business School Press, 1989); Thomas J. Peters and Robert H. Waterrnan, Jr., *In Search of Excellence* (New York: Warner Books, 1982); and J. M. Bums, *Leadership* (New York: Harper and Row, 1978) are only three of many who recognize this complexity.

[14] Joseph L. Badaracco, Jr. and Richard R. Ellsworth, *Leadership and the Quest for Integrity* (Boston: Harvard Business School Press, 1989).

[15] J. M. Burns, *Leadership* (New York: Harper and Row, 1978):20.

[16] Hersey and Blanchard, 1988:202–226.

[17] Dennis H. Wrong, *Power—Its Forms, Bases and Uses* (New York: Harper and Row, 1980):24.

[18] Hersey and Blanchard list seven kinds of power including expert, information, referent, legitimate, reward, connection and coercive (1989: 214–217).

[19] Ted Ward. "Servants, Leaders and Tyrants," *Missions and Theological Education in World Perspective*, Harvie M. Conn and Samuel F. Rowen (eds.) (Farmington, MI: Associates of Urbanus, 1984):19–40.

[20] The name of the church is withheld because it is not my intention to embarrass either the pastoral staff or the members of that congregation.

21 Current "contingency" leadership theories describe the complex and dynamic interactive relationships among the leader, follower(s) and situation. Each contributes to the other two. The leader through patterned behavior or style influences followers in a structured context toward a goal which benefits both and the wider context. The followers allocate the right to be influenced to the leader and provide the benefits of social recognition and goal achievement for him/her. The situation provides the organizational and social structures, worldview and values which both constrain, guide and facilitate the influence process.

22 J. Robert Clinton, "Leadership Emergence Patterns," Unpublished manuscript, 1986:14.

23 Ward, 1984.

24 J. Robert Clinton, *The Making of a Leader* (Colorado Springs: NavPress, 1988):127.

25 Lawrence O. Richards, *A Theology of Christian Education* (Grand Rapids: Zondervan Publishing House, 1975):231.

26 Geert Hofstede, "Motivation, Leadership, and Organization: Do American Theories Apply Abroad?" *Organizational Dynamics*, Summer, 1980:42–62.

27 Hofstede, p. 45.

28 Hofstede, p. 45.

29 Hofstede, p. 45.

30 Hofstede, p. 45.

31 Hofstede, p. 46.

32 Donald A. McGavran in 1969 described five kinds of leaders needed for growing churches in a lectureship at Columbia Bible College in Columbia, S.C. Edgar J. Elliston and W. Michael Smith in "An Outline for Program Planning and Evaluation" (an unpublished manuscript) described a leadership training program around five kinds of leaders in 1976. Lois McKinney, "Training Leaders" in Virgil Gerber, *Discipline Through Theological Education by Extension* (Chicago: Moody Press, 1980) and J. Robert Clinton, *Leadership Training Models Manual* (Unpublished manuscript, 1984) have variously described five kinds of leaders who are needed for the church community.

33 It should be noted that while the number five serves as a useful way to classify the types of leaders, a local situation may in fact require a different number. Furthermore, the ways that leaders are classified may require a very different kind of classification system because of the

cultural situation. For example, leaders could be classified into prophet, priestly and kingly categories in terms of their functioning. The lexical categories in a given language will also condition how leadership should be classified.

34   Single-cell congregations generally peak at about 200 members.

35   See also Donald A. McGavran and Win Am, *How to Grow A Church* (Glendale, CA: Regal, 1974):89–97, Elliston and Smith 1976, McKinney 1980.

36   David Rambo, "Patterns of Bible Institute Training Overseas," "Theological Education by Extension: What is it Accomplishing?" "Crisis at the Top: Training High Level Leaders," "Leadership for the Cities: Facing the Urban Mandate," 1981 Church Growth Lectures, Fuller Theological Seminary.

37   Adapted from Edgar J. Elliston (ed.), *Christian Relief and Development: Training Leaders for Effective Ministry* (Dallas: Word Books 1989): 190.

38   James M. Kouzes and Barry Z. Posner, *The Leadership Challenge How to Get Extraordinary Things Done in Organizations* (San Francisco: Jossey-Bass Publishers, 1987):310.

39   Edwin Hollander, *Leadership Dynamics*. (New York: The Free Press, 1978).

40   Cf. Yukl 1989: 231–214 and Edgar Schein, *Organizational Culture and Leadership* (San Francisco: Jossey-Bass).

CHAPTER THREE

VALUES FOR CHRISTIAN LEADERS

The coffee was getting cold as Pastor James continued to question his friend and colleague Paulo. "What decisions should we make? Who should we select to be trained? What content is essential? Who should advise in the design and implementation of the program? When should the training be done? How should the spiritual formation issue be addressed? What standards should we seek to attain . . . ?"

Paulo responded, "All of your questions keep going back to value issues. Where do we find the answers to what we 'should' do?"

These questions could have arisen in Colombo, Sri Lanka, Columbus, Ohio or Cairo, Egypt. These questions emerge in urban, rural and traditional settings whether the church has grown to ten or ten thousand.

Values provide the shared roadways on which leaders exercise their influence and followers respond. While driving I am always aware of the road and continually correct my driving to the road. While other conditions such as the weather, traffic congestion, my own vehicle and its condition and load affect my driving, the road provides a primary set of directional constraints. Many variables affect leadership effectiveness, yet values provide the constraints for all of them. Leadership effectiveness depends on many influences, but values provide the paths for these influences. Effective influence toward shared goals depends upon integrity to these values.

Shared values provide the criteria for what ought to be done and what ought not to be done.

Values provide both the guidelines and constraints for making judgments at every juncture. These values will come from at least two critically important perspectives: 1) Revealed values found in Scripture provide the normative base for and equipping of the selection and employment of power for influencing the selection of leaders; 2) cultural values found in the broader culture and the immediate sub-culture of the church, agency or community provided the initial guidelines.

It is beyond the scope of this text to either seek to identify or describe the meaning of identifying local cultural values. However, if the leadership development approach suggested in this book is followed, local values will be naturally incorporated into the formation of home grown leaders.

The purpose of this chapter is to identify the basic biblical values that pastors and informed church leaders should apply in their own leading, the equipping of others to lead and the evaluation of leadership generally in their situation.

Biblical values undergird selection criteria, the development processes, the bases for evaluation of spiritual leadership and the selection and employment of power. These values fit interculturally with only the specific local forms changing as the values are expressed. They serve as the criteria for judging how well or appropriately a spiritual leader functions.

Biblical Bases of Leadership Development

Scripture writers use a variety of words to express the concepts which relate to leadership selection and development. While the contexts provide the perspectives to interpret these words, the words themselves provide useful insights into the selection and development of spiritual leaders.

"Selection" Words

The writers of Scripture use more than twenty words to describe the act of selection or the process of selection for leadership. The implications of these words provide a useful range of insight to understand how spiritual leaders were selected along with some of the undergirding values for the selection. Often, the context explicitly describes the process and values, but attention to the words used adds further insight.

Selection in the Old Testament

The most frequently used word for selection in the Old Testament is the Hebrew word *bachar*. It appears about 120 times. This word means to "choose after testing." Conventional wisdom also supports the idea that leaders should be ones chosen at least on the basis of proven competency and motivation or commitment.

Selection in the New Testament

The New Testament writers use a wider range of Greek words to describe the selection of leaders. In the English translations these words are not always distinguishable because several Greek words may be translated by the same English word or one Greek word may be translated by several English words and the English words overlap.

The New Testament writers frequently use the word *kaleo* (call) and a related word, *prokaleo* (call to or toward). Often this "calling" indicates a selection or choice. The selection contains a directionality "from" and "to," suggesting a purpose. Other choice-related words include *hairetizo* (to lift), *haireomai* (lift for oneself), *eklego* (lay out), *epilego* (lay open), and *stratolego* (enlist).

The importance of the selection of leaders is repeatedly underscored in Scripture. The selection process brings different elements into brighter focus as different leaders are considered. In David's selection, for example, the character of his heart was brought into focus. Jesus' selection of His disciples followed a night of prayer. The selection of Barnabas and Saul at Antioch brought together a discernment of the leading of the Holy Spirit and an affirmation of the Antioch church.

While integrity is always important, and the qualifications, commitment, situation, status and other traits are often brought into focus, another consistent, essential component in the selection process is "God's calling." God called Noah directly. Joseph received visions and dreams. David was selected from his brothers by an incredulous Samuel. God clearly called Isaiah, Daniel, Ezekiel, Jonah, Amos, Hosea and Nehemiah from very different situations and backgrounds of experience to very different leadership ministries.

The selection always related to the leadership/ministry to be done. "Generic" selection is unknown. God chooses women and men for specific ministries.

We can see from Scripture the importance given to the selection of leaders. It was always a Spirit-led process—something in which God was actively involved. The forms of the involvement varied from a direct confrontation such as Moses had to the casting of lots with Matthias. The choice was always with a purpose. Joseph was chosen to preserve his family in Egypt. Moses was chosen to lead the Israelites to freedom. Joshua was chosen to lead the Hebrew people into Canaan and get them settled. Gideon's task was smaller, but no less demanding. Saul was selected with a clear purpose to bring the Gentiles to light. Titus was selected and commissioned to serve the church in Crete with a clear purpose.

The selection of leaders frequently involved the equipping participation of other leaders. Moses worked with Joshua. Samuel anointed Saul and later David. Elijah worked with Elisha. Jesus chose His disciples and then equipped them. The disciples then helped select others. Leaders involved in selection and equipping were occasionally surpassed by their followers. Look at Barnabas and Saul. Look at Jesus' disciples. He never traveled beyond the narrow confines of Palestine except for a brief period as a refugee in Egypt. Yet, His disciples reached west beyond Rome, south to Alexandria and Ethiopia, north into Turkey and east to South India.

The "selection" of "volunteers" requires careful attention. Little is said about "volunteers" as leaders in the Scriptures. Men and women are called and then expected to "volunteer." Ministry opportunities, gifts and obligations are given to each believer so each one is expected to "volunteer." However, to seek volunteers outside of their "calling" or "giftedness" will likely prove not only to be less than fulfilling for them, but will likely result in frustration and "burn-out." Volunteers who serve out of their giftedness will likely find fulfillment and can be expected to have much longer-term commitments. Other people will observe their effectiveness.

The selection of leaders is a crucial element in the development of men and women to lead. However, it is not enough. We must also give careful attention to the entrusting of commitment, legitimation of and educational development of Christian leaders.

"Committal" Words

Another set of words which focuses on the commitment and empowerment aspects of the selection include *didomi* (give, commit, deliver), *paradidomi* (give over), *tithemi* (place, put, set, commit, appoint, ordain, give), *paratithemi* (put along side of, commit to, entrust to for safe keeping or transmission), and *pisteuo* (trust in, confide in, commit to).

The practical application of these committal ideas may be seen in the biblical metaphors used to describe follower-leaders. A servant is one to whom both tasks and relationships have been entrusted. The servant "serves" as a "trustee" (steward) who is "appointed" or "given" to accomplish what has been "placed" in his or her hands. The shepherd typically is entrusted with the sheep which are not his "personally," but belong to his father or family. He is "committed to care for, protect, nurture, guide and know the sheep not only by his own voice, but by the "chief shepherd" or owner of the sheep. He is not a "hireling" but a member of the family who has a personal interest in the sheep. The father and family place their confidence or trust in the shepherd, because their livelihood depends on him.

The apostle Paul entrusted the care of congregations in several places to Timothy (e.g., Philippi—Ph 2:9–24; Thessalonica—1 Thess 3:2–3; and Corinth—1 Cor 4:17; 16:10–11).

"Legitimation" Words

Another set of words is involved in the legitimation of the leadership selection. Some of these words include *yasad* (lay, lay a foundation, appoint, settle), *amad* (cause to stand), *kathistemi* (place or set down), *krino* (judge or decide), *horizo* (mark out or off), *poieo* (do or make), and *tithemi* (put, place, sit).

The charge to both the leader and followers as part of the legitimating process occurs in many places in Scripture. Three examples occur with Joshua (Nu 27:18ff; De 31:7ff; and Jos 1:1–9) and Jesus' disciples (Mt 10:5–15; Mk 6:11–42; and Lk 10:1–16).

Legitimation relates to the empowerment and the establishment of authority to influence. The apostle Paul legitimized Timothy as his personal envoy, thus empowering him with a delegated authority in an appropriate status (e.g., 1 Cor 4:17; 16:10–11; Phil 2:19–24). Legitimation may be done individually or corporately, as was done with the church in Jerusalem in their "sending" Barnabas to Antioch (Acts 11:22) or by the church in Antioch sending Barnabas and Saul to Cyprus (Acts 13:1–3). In all of these examples, the primary source of authority or legitimacy was not either the individual or the believing community, but God through the Holy Spirit. In legitimizing his disciples' world-wide ministry Jesus said, "All authority in heaven and earth is mine, therefore go make disciples of all nations . . ." (Mt 2:18–20).

"Educational" Words

When Jesus selected His disciples, He had several options available to equip His disciples. The Jews had formal educational means available in the synagogue schools. Paul was formally trained as a Pharisee by Gamaliel. Greek schools were also well known. However, Jesus did not chose schools as the primary model to equip His followers to become leaders. That approach would not be followed until later in the life of the church. He chose rather a nonformal mix of dialogue, experience and reflection.

Three Hebrew words provide clues to a holistic view of learning which characterized Jesus development style. The word *bin*, for example, means "to cause to understand, discern, attend, or consider." Parables given in context and explanations of events were Jesus' typical mode of instruction. *Sakal*, while translated "to teach," suggests a causing to act wisely or to guide. Jesus modeled what He expected of His disciples, deliberately calling attention to His way. *Yasar*, in addition to meaning "teach," may also mean "to instruct, chasten, or reform." Jesus' purpose was clearly aimed at changing or transforming His disciples.

Six New Testament words provide additional important insights. *Didasko* occurs most frequently. It simply means "to teach or instruct," implying the imparting of both knowledge and skills. The word suggests the bridging between the teacher and the learner. It is used for the impartation of both practical or theoretical knowledge.

Katartizo further enriches our understanding. It is variously translated as "to equip, fit, adjust thoroughly, perfect, frame, make perfect, mend, restore, train and prepare." The concept drives toward developing maturation into proper relationships for a perfect fit.[1]

The word *matheteo* (to disciple) suggests the enrollment of a learner as an apprentice under the discipline of another. A disciple is one who "directs his mind to something."[2] The focus is not on one's competency, but on his/her commitment to learning and adoption of the specific knowledge or conduct. The disciple emerges "according to a set plan."[3]

Paideuo is variously translated as "train, instruct, nurture, cultivate and chasten." *Probabazo* means "to go up before" or "to instruct."

Gumnazo suggests disciplined training for an athletic event, but is used to refer to training for godliness (1 Tim 4:7) or training for good and evil (He 5:14).

From these words we can see the focus is not just on the mastery of content, but on a broader development in which one is transformed, informed and equipped to function. Again, we must see that the development is more than just aimed at skilled functioning. It goes beyond to relationships and the character of the person. It does not occur in a once-for-all training program, but rather is seen as a lifetime developmental process.

The Selection and Use of Power

Effective leadership is by definition the effective use of power. All leaders use power to lead. The use of power is not at issue. However, what kinds of power and the extent to which each kind is used is an issue. One's values again both guide and constrain the selection and use of power.

Christian leaders have three basic kinds of power available to use. These three kinds of power are much more closely interlinked than many people in the West imagine. The appropriate, balanced use of these three kinds of power lead to effective leadership. The mis-use or mis-appropriation of any of these three will ultimately lead to dysfunctionality not only of the leader, but the followers as well.

Physical Power

The first kind of power is physical power such as is studied in physics. While physical strength and power is employed by leaders, it is not our primary focus.

Social Power

The second kind of power is social power. This kind of potential for influence between persons is studied in the "social sciences" such as sociology, psychology, anthropology, political science, history, economics and the like.

Often social power has been divided into two categories since the Italian author Machiavelli: fear and love. Fear relates to positional power. Love relates to the person.

These two categories of power have been further divided by contemporary management authors. Hersey and Blanchard, for example, divide this kind of power into seven categories.

Spiritual Power

The third and most important kind of power available to Christian leaders is spiritual power. Spiritual power has its source in God. The normal employment of spiritual power is in all three power domains: physical, social and spiritual. God is the primary source of spiritual power. His power is creative and builds relationships toward eternal life. Counterfeited spiritual power is available from Satan. It is limited and counterfeits the power of God. Satanic power is destructive, deceptive, disruptive, damaging, discrediting, isolative, selfish, impatient, accusatory, lacking in hope and lacking in joy. It leads to death, destruction and ultimate alienation.

Every follower of Jesus Christ may be empowered by the Holy Spirit to do the works He did (Jn 14:12–13). The marks or characteristics of this empowerment to lead or influence other people distinguish Christians from others who may use other kinds of power. Richard Foster suggest seven "marks of spiritual power."[4] This set of characteristics is not intended to be comprehensive, rather suggestive of the key facets of spiritual power.

Love

Spiritual power is the potential for influence used for the good of others without regard to the cost to oneself or for one's own personal advantage.

Humility

Humility or meekness is "power under control." Spiritual power is not a personal possession, perquisite or right, but rather a gift which the "holder" is to control, steward and use for the purpose of God Himself. Spiritual power, then, should be demonstrated in a spirit of humility and meekness.

Self-limitation

The spiritual power holder limits his/her use of that power to God's purposes.

Joy

The person who is empowered with spiritual power will be joyful. The joy is not a surface level slap-stick humor nor happiness which depends on the immediate situation, but a deep level joy based on hope in the assurance of the final outcomes.

Vulnerability

Spiritual power influences from a position of apparent weakness and vulnerability. Organizational status and personal charisma are not relevant.

Submission

Submission to God allows His power to flow through a person. Foster writes,

> There is a power that comes through spiritual gifts, and there is a power that comes through spiritual positioning. The two work in unison. Submission gives us spiritual positioning. We are positioned under the leadership of Christ and under the authority of others. We find others in the Christian Fellowship who can further us in the things of God. We submit to Scripture to learn more perfectly the ways of God with human beings. We submit to the Holy Spirit to learning the meaning of obedience. We submit to the life of faith in order to understand the difference between human power and divine power."[5]

Freedom

Spiritual power frees men and women from sickness, demonization and from error. Spiritual power frees a person so he/she can respond with an unconditional commitment to Jesus Christ as Lord. All of these characteristics of power are demonstrated in Jesus Christ as He is described in Phil 2:5–11.

The results of spiritual power in the life of a person may be seen in the effects/results in a person's life, i.e., fruit of the

Spirit: love, joy, peace, patience, kindness, gentleness, goodness, self-control as the person employs the gift(s) of the Spirit in his/her life.

Spiritual authority, like other forms of authority, is both "delegated" and "allocated." Spiritual authority is the right to employ spiritual power.

It is delegated from God.

The right to use spiritual power is given by God in the forms of spiritual gifts (e.g., apostleship, evangelist, prophet, pastor-teacher, hospitality, liberality, helps, administration, leadership, faith, tongues, interpretation of tongues, healings, discernment, wisdom). It is accessible through prayer, praise and meditation. It is a Christian's right to use it in praise, intercession, or blessing.

Spiritual power is evident in the effects it has internally—in terms of the fruit of the Spirit—love, joy, peace, patience, kindness, gentleness, goodness, self-control. It is also evident in the effects it has externally in the lives of others.

Delegated spiritual power is sovereignly given by God through the Holy Spirit so—

a. we can "stand" (Eph 6:12–18).
b. we can "disciple all the nations" (Mt 28:18–20)
c. we can "bind" and "loose" using the keys that Jesus promised Peter in the establishing the church. The doors/gates of hell cannot prevail against this power.

As Christians we are prohibited from using some forms of spiritual power, e.g., curses, engaging in satanic rituals, witchcraft, the occult, necromancy, and the like.

Spiritual authority is allocated or recognized by other people and spirits. Spiritual authority is allocated by the people who are willing to be influenced, that is, it is recognized and allowed. It may be legitimized privately. It may be legitimized in public ceremonies such as "ordination" and the "laying on of hands."

A person's spiritual authority is recognized in the spiritual realm. Jesus said, "Whenever two or three of you agree about anything . . . it will be done." (Mt 18:19) When elders (who have spiritual authority) pray, results can be expected (James 5:17). People who are demonized are led to freedom by confronting the evil spirits and taking away their bases for influencing a person by people who use spiritual authority granted by the Lord through His Spirit.

The same set of biblical values serves to guide and constrain all three kinds of power. The primary value is repeated numerous times in the New Testament both in the teaching of Jesus as He cited the Old Testament (Deut 6:5) and in the teaching of the apostles. The primary value is love—first of God with all of one's heart, soul, mind and strength, and then of the other person (Lu 10:27–37). Jesus stated that all of the law and prophets is made complete in love. John clearly taught that love of God and the other person is absolutely required. The use of all of the spiritual gifts is to be guided and constrained by love according to the apostle Paul (1 Cor 13). Love prevents using any kinds of power for one's personal advantage.

A second value related to power is the purpose toward which power is to be directed. Jesus claimed "all authority," that is, the right to use all power in heaven and earth (Mt 28:18–19). On the basis of that authority His disciples are commanded to disciple/make disciples of all nations by going, baptizing and teaching obedience in all things He commanded (Mt 28:18–20). The value addressed here is one of purpose and goal. Our influence should contribute toward the accomplishment of this purpose.

Whether physical, social or spiritual power is involved, these two primary values provide directional constraint.

Values also serve as constraints with the use of power (proscriptions of what "ought not" to be done). Power ought not be employed for personal advantage. Power should not be employed for the personal disadvantage of others. Appropriateness of the kind of spiritual power to employ may be seen in the relationship of the task at hand to the kingdom of God. One should assume the beginning point is the employment of spiritual power.

New Testament Bases for Leading

The primary values for Christian leadership are found in the New Testament. The key person is Jesus Himself. He taught and exemplified the ideal of what was to be expected of Christian leadership. The apostles Peter and James both provide case studies and teaching for developing bases for Christian leadership. The apostle Paul both as an example and as a teacher provides much additional insight into the values, principles and expectations for Christian leadership. Moving back from a christocentric model, the Old Testament provides an additional wealth of insight and information with both positive and negative examples.

The basic model for Christian leadership is servanthood. *Servanthood* provides a different way of looking at the concept of a differentiated role. This theme grows out of firmly established roots in the Old Testament patriarchs, prophets, priests and kings. The New Testament authors develop the ideas about servanthood from a variety of views to fill in a very complex picture.[6]

The picture of the servant leader begins to take shape through the major prophets (Isaiah, Jeremiah, Ezekiel and Daniel). Jesus then fills in the details of the picture through His life and teachings. Then in the early church, the apostles demonstrate and amplify what it means to be a servant leader. Beginning with the prophets, continuing in the life and ministry of Jesus and then through the leaders of the early church God can be seen to initiate four activities to place a person in service. He calls, cleanses, commissions and empowers for service. God continues to reaffirm these actions and adds to them preservation and guidance in service. The servant responds simply with humility in faith and obedience. Finally, the Lord vindicates His servant with victory. From the calling to the vindication the authority is the Lord's and the servant simply seeks to obey while influencing as he/she is led.[7] Through the gospel accounts about thirty-five different images or metaphors are used to describe the disciples as emerging leaders. The focus is on their obedience, faith, and learning to follow. Significantly, terms related to power and position are not only missing, but are criticized by Jesus when brought into focus.

The New Testament writers portray rich and complex pictures of Christians in ministry as they serve and lead. Christian writers have categorized these leadership ideas as taught and demonstrated in the New Testament which reflect their own categories of leadership. One may legitimately see different types of leaders as described in this book. One may also describe leaders in terms of local (elders and deacons) or itinerant (apostles and evangelists). One may also interpret both the fruit of the Spirit and the gifts of the Spirit in terms of vocation. One only need observe how Paul defined Timothy's qualifications in his letters to Corinth or the ways he described spiritual gifts in Rom 12 and 1 Cor 11. The following treatment of leadership in the New Testament does not attempt to be comprehensive, but rather suggestive.

What does not appear in the New Testament is the sharp status and role distinctions between the "clergy" and "laity" which exist in some Christian communities today. Jesus and the Eleven were all "laymen" in terms of formal theological education and "ordination." Only the apostle Paul had a formal theological education. However, even he had to have a year of inservice training in Antioch before he could be sent out under the supervision of Barnabas. Rather, all of these leaders were seen as God's people (laity) and all were called (clergy) to serve. A serious risk we face today is reading back into the New Testament account our own perspectives.

Jesus' Leadership Expectations

Jesus provides the normative case study for Christian leadership. The key feature of Jesus' leadership was servanthood. He saw himself as a servant. "For who is greater, the one who reclines at table, or the one who serves? Is it not the one who reclines at table? But I am among you as the one who serves" (Lk 22:27).

Jesus described himself as one who was to "minister" or serve others. He washed the feet of his disciples to demonstrate that he expected the leaders of his people not to be proud and "lord it over" others (Jn 13:3–17). Jesus' teachings which relates to leadership clearly show his servant-ministry ideal.

> For I gave you an example that you also should do as I did to you. Truly, truly, I say to you, a slave is not greater than his master; neither one who is sent greater than the one who sent him. If you know these things, you are blessed if you do them (Jn 13:15–17).

His service consisted largely of teaching and healing (e.g., Mt 8:14; Lk 7:2; 8:41; Mt 5–7, 13:37; 24:33). All of his teaching and healings addressed social, physical and spiritual issues. His power base was invariably spiritual.

The words "leader" and "leadership" do not appear in the gospels. Bennett asks, Why is this? Could it be that leadership has more to do with learning to follow than learning to command, supervise or manage? Could it be that effective leadership depends more on right attitudes than on mastery of certain skills? Could it be that it is more important for the leader to understand what he or she has in common with other followers of the Lord than to focus on what sets the leader apart from the rest?[8]

When the mother of James and John, the sons of Zebedee, came to him requesting special leadership status for them, Jesus refused. After the other ten had heard about this request, they were indignant about the request for special status. Jesus then spoke pointedly about their status and expected relationships with each other. Jesus specifically prohibits the two common traits of leaders in secular situations: "lording it over others" and "exercising authority" over others. The phrase "their great ones exercise authority over them" carries the idea of tyrannizing one's subjects [9] especially by the misuse of social and physical forms of power. This attitude toward leadership was not new with Jesus. Samuel had reprimanded Saul about his disobedience, self-seeking rebelliousness and arrogance in his leadership (1 Sam 15:22–23).

While terms of power and authority are used to describe
Jesus in the gospels, it is important to note that these kinds of
words are never used to apply to the disciples in the gospels.
None is called "bishop," "lord," "teacher," "administrator" or
"leader." Jesus' intention for his disciples was that they be good
followers.

Jesus showed his disciples how to follow, how to obey,
how to respond to the authority and call of God. He demonstrated how to use spiritual power. He knew that the effective
leader must first learn how to be a faithful follower. Jesus also
knew how destructive the attitudes of pride and ambition could
be within the community of disciples. Therefore, he taught them
attitudes of humility and self-sacrifice, using the image of the
servant, and reminded them of their equal standing before God
as brothers. Jesus wanted his disciples to think of themselves as
"among" one another, as brothers, and "under" one another, as
servants, more than "over," as those in authority.[10]

Jesus' Criticism of Inappropriate Leadership

Jesus severely criticized the strict religious leaders of his day
who had been deeply affected by the status-seeking, hierarchical
and secularizing background of Hellenistic influence.[11] This
criticism provides further insight into Jesus' intentions by
showing what was not acceptable.

Jesus clearly exposes both the leadership styles to be
avoided and by contrast those elements of leadership which
should characterize Christian leaders. Jesus thoroughly criticized
the religious leaders for leadership which moves away from a
servant orientation.

> Then Jesus spoke to the multitudes and to His disci-
> ples, saying, "The scribes and the Pharisees have
> seated themselves in the chair of Moses; therefore all
> that they tell you, do and observe, but do not do
> according to their deeds; for they say things, and do
> not do them. And they tie up heavy loads, and lay
> them on men's shoulders; but they themselves are
> unwilling to move them with so much as a finger.
> But they do all their deeds to be noticed by men; for

they broaden their phylacteries, and lengthen the tassels of their garments. And they love the place of honor at banquets, and the chief seats in the synagogues, and respectful greetings in the market places, and being called by men, Rabbi. But do not be called Rabbi; for One is your Teacher, and you are all brothers. And do not call anyone on earth your father; for One is your Father, He who is in heaven. And do not be called leaders; for One is your Leader, that is, Christ. But the greatest among you shall be your servant. And whoever exalts himself shall be humbled; and whoever humbles himself shall be exalted (Mt 23:1–12).

Ward observed,

Leadership for the church is to be non-tyrannical servanthood, evaluated in the light of the teachings of our Lord. Let us therefore accept the evaluative criteria of Matthew 23:1–12. Verse 3: Let us reconcile word and deed. Verse 4: Let us not be delegative but participatory. Verse 5: Let us seek no exalted status. Verse 6: Let us accept no special privilege. Verse 7: Let us take no pride from secular recognition. Verse 8: Let us reject titles of authority, preferring instead a simple relationship as brothers. Verse 9: Let us develop *real* relationships, not artificial and titular relationships. Verse 10: Let us share with all God's people the recognition of one master. Verse 11: Let us relate as servants to the needs of others. Verse 12: Let us live in humble life-style.[12]

Jesus' Example

Jesus exemplified these ten characteristics in his leadership for people who would follow him. The apostle Paul wrote,

Have this attitude in yourselves which was also in Christ Jesus who, although He existed in the form of God, did not regard equality with God a thing to be

grasped, but emptied Himself, taking the form of a
bond-servant, and being made in the likeness of
men. And being found in appearance as a man, He
humbled himself by becoming obedient to the point
of death, even death on a cross (Phil 2:5-8).

Jesus summarized his leadership expectations by saying,
"Whoever wishes to be great among you shall be your servant.
Whoever wishes to be first among you shall be your slave" (Mt
20:27).

Jesus also emphasized the quality of serving as a fundamen-
tal characteristic of such a ministry. Again, he pointed to himself
as the model and example. "I am among you as one who serves"
(Lk 22:27; cf. Jn 13:13–15). "If anyone serves me, he must
follow me; and where I am, there shall my servant be also; if
anyone serves me, the Father will honor him" (Jn 12:26).

Jesus sought to help his disciples learn that they were being
called into a unique set of relationships with each other, with
other disciples, with nonbelievers and with God. These relationships would be evaluated by their love for each other, their personal commitment to Jesus and their faithfulness in carrying out
their assigned ministries or tasks.

In addition to his focus on relationships, Jesus also emphasized the task to which the disciples were being called. They
were called to be servants of each other and of the Lord. To
emphasize these two complementary teachings of relationships
and an orientation to the task at hand, Jesus used at least thirty-
five different metaphors to bring out the nuances he intended.[13]

The Apostle Paul's Expectations

The leadership perspective and expectations of the apostle
Paul support both what Jesus taught and exemplified. When
Paul wrote about leadership matters, he saw leadership as service, but not as related to any hierarchical status. In his own
ministry he did not seek to build relationships on his own learning or religious status, but rather as one who was also seeking to
serve Jesus Christ (Phil 3:3–11). Paul cited his own example of
leadership seven times and called others to emulate him as a

leader.[14] In the selection of leaders he was concerned about their total behavior, experience and ability, not their rank.

Paul emphasized a distributive leadership among the people of God based on gifts or God-given abilities rather than on an authoritarian hierarchical structure. Paul held that the various leaders are essentially equal even though their functions differ. This emphasis appears in his analogy of the church as a body with many different functioning parts (1 Co 12:12–27). The purpose for every kind of leadership was for the building up of the church (1 Co 12:2–7; Eph 4:11).

Both in his own example and in his teaching the apostle Paul's expectations for leadership coincide with the criteria described by Jesus in Mt 23:1–12. Paul lived as an example of what he taught (Phil 4:8–9; Ac 20:17–27; 1 Co 11:1). He sought not just to tell others what to do, but to participate with them as an example (Phil 3:17). His acceptance of Onesimus and his urging Philemon is an example (Phm 8–22). Paul considered leadership as that which should bind the church together in service, not as something which splits the church into status-seeking parties (1 Co 9:13, 3:3–11). In these passages the only leader who has any status is Jesus Himself (v. 11). Paul did not seek or rely on the privilege of being an apostle (Ac 20:33–35; 1 Co 9:13–15; 1 The 2:9; 2 The 3:8). From these passages we know that he maintained a simple lifestyle. Paul did not seek either secular or religious recognition after his conversion (Phil 3:4–11).

Paul's instruction about spiritual gifts further clarifies Jesus' teaching about leadership and its interdependent servant quality. His instructions to and for elders and deacons provide further insights into the qualities and other leadership values Jesus began to teach. One could take individual epistles such as 2 Corinthians and discern additional values. Topical studies which relate to leadership, such as spiritual gifts, are critical to understand Christian leadership. Situational studies such as at Antioch, Jerusalem, Ephesus, Philippi and Corinth provide additional examples and insights. Tracing the interpersonal relationships with a view to learning leadership values provides another rich mine. Such relationships as Barnabas and Paul,

Paul and Timothy, and Paul and Philemon are only three of many instructive relationships.

Both by example in his reproof of Peter and Barnabas (Gal 2:11–14) and by his written invitation for correction to the church in Galatia, the apostle Paul taught that leaders—even apostles—were to be held accountable by the church. If the highest level of leader departs from the basic teachings, the church was instructed to ostracize them. Paul's clear teaching reflects Jesus' teaching that no servant is above his master, but must remain accountable, obedient and subject to correction. Paul defines the scope and purpose of this correction in describing the usefulness of scriptures to Timothy who was an internationally known and respected church leader when he received that letter (cf. 2 Tim 3:14–17).

For the purpose of this chapter the basic leadership lessons from the writings about elders, deacons and spiritual gifts will re-enforce the primary values for Christian leaders as seen in the life and teachings of Jesus.

Elders

The term "elders," *presbuteroi*, suggests both the qualities of old age and experience (Ac 14:23; 20:17; 1 Ti 5:17; Tit 1:5; 1 Pe 5:1–3). They are referred to as overseers (*episkopoi*) where the Greek culture was more influential than the Hebrew (Ac 20:28; 1 Ti 3:1, 2 and Tit 1:7). Knox writes,

> The term "elder" seems equivalent to "bishop"; and it is not unlikely that the word, *episkopos*, ("bishop") was sometimes used to make intelligible to Gentiles the meaning of *presbyteros* ("elder"), which would have sounded strange to them . . .[15]

Therefore, while the meaning varies somewhat, the terms "elder" and "bishop" were dynamic equivalents between the Jewish and Greek congregations.[16] The elders or bishops provided the primary leadership for local congregations during the first century. Values applied to the elders were applicable even more widely to other leaders.

Qualifications of an Elder

The key qualifications for elders—leaders—are Christian maturity and being above reproach (integrity) in their community (1 Ti 3:2). Paul lists related qualifications in his first letter to Timothy (3:2–7) and suggests a similar set of qualifications to Titus (Tit 1:5–9).

Expected Elder Responsibilities

It is not possible to construct a list of all of the possible leadership responsibilities of the elders. However, it is possible to gain insight from some scriptural suggestions: 1) hold "forth the faithful word" (Ti 1:9; 1 Ti 6:35); 2) teach the faith (1 Ti 3:2); 3) extend hospitality (Tit 1:8; 1 Ti 3:2); 4) exhort in sound doctrine (Tit 1:9); 5) "refute those who contradict" (Ti 1:9); 6) manage his own household (1 Ti 3; 4–5); 7) exemplify the faith (1 Pe 5:3) and provide general oversight (Ac 20:28; 1 Ti 5:17; 1 Pe 5:2–3).

Elders' Leadership Style

Peter succinctly describes his expectations for the elders' leadership style: a) They ought to serve/shepherd the flock voluntarily, not because they are forced to do so. b) They ought to serve eagerly, not for the personal gain they may receive. c) They ought to be examples and not lord it over the flock. d) Their relationship with everyone ought to be characterized by humility, not pride (cf. 1 Pe 5:1–5).

Elders, then, are to be experienced and mature Christians who have demonstrated that they are capable of leading their families and who are above reproach in their communities. They ought to be irreproachable, and exhibit self-control and good will toward others. They are expected to know the Christian faith and be able to both teach and defend it. They are expected to be shepherding servants.

Deacons

The word "deacon" is a transliteration of the Greek word *diakonos*, which means "servant" or "minister." Every elder or other Christian leader is expected to be a deacon, that is, one who serves (cf. Mt 20:26–27; 23:10–11). The term "deacon" as it refers to Christian leaders is used both for men and women (cf. Rom 16:1; 1 Ti 3:8). Deacons do what needs to be done, whether it be serving tables (Ac 6:1–6), teaching or evangelizing (Ac 8:26ff).

In his first letter to Timothy the apostle Paul writes about deacons (3:8–13). From these brief accounts at least the following qualifications may be seen which applied to the selection of those first deacons and presumably to those who would be chosen later: 1) dignified, that is, having a sense of gravity and reverence; 2) honest, not "double-tongued," insincere or talebearers; 3) not drunkards; 4) not materialistic or greedy for gain; 5) committed believers, "full of the Spirit"; 6) having already demonstrated their commitment to serve; 7) monogamous; 8) good managers of their children and their own households; and 9) wise. Wisdom signifies that ability to distinguish between what is advantageous and what is harmful, rightly to assess a situation and to act in such a way as to bring intention to fulfillment. Wisdom signifies the right use of knowledge.

Spiritual Gifts

The apostle Paul gives three principal lists of spiritual gifts to the churches in Rome, Corinth and Ephesus. Each list differs, although some overlapping emerges with the gifts of apostle, prophet and teacher. In each case the purpose of the spiritual gifts is to build or strengthen the body of the church. The reason for his writing to each of the churches about the variety of gifts was to stress the function of the gifts within the whole community. Paul, writing to the church in Corinth (1 Co 12–14), places much emphasis on the employing of the various gifts for the common good and the kind or quality of relationships which characterize those who exercise their spiritual God-given abilities or gifts. Spiritual gifts provide one important means through which God influences His people. Spiritual gifts are one means by which spiritual power is employed. Christian leadership or the process of influencing toward God's purpose is greatly facilitated through the use of spiritual gifts.

If leadership relates to ministry or serving, then these spiritual gifts must certainly relate to leadership. If a leader is one with a differentiated role, then these gifts must be considered in the context of leadership. These gifts relate to many ministry functions. Leadership is ministry within the church. Many kinds of ministries are required for a healthy church, just as different kinds of leaders are needed. The gifts relate to every type or kind of leader.

Classifying spiritual gifts in four categories helps one understand both their functions in the church and their impact on one's understanding of Christian leadership. All of the gifts are given for the common good. These four categories of gifts serve to explain part of what the Lord is doing. However, these categories of gifts are not limited to a particular type or kind of leader.

Special gifts (*domata*) relate specifically to the gifts Jesus gave (Eph 4:7–13). These special gifts relate specifically to leadership functions in the Body. These gifts include: 1) apostles— the "sent ones" with special delegated authority from God and allocated spiritual authority from the people of God to establish the church in new places; 2) prophets who "speak before." The prophets speak forth from God, interpreting his message and will in the present context. Occasionally, their message has a future foretelling character; 3) evangelists who serve as midwives bringing people the message of the gospel and assisting in their delivery into the kingdom of God; and 4) pastor-teachers who conserve, nurture and lead the church on to the multiplication. In each kind of leader the servant character, the trustee or steward's accountability and the shepherd's concern for the health and growth of the whole are evident.

A second category of spiritual gifts (*charismata*) are speaking or word gifts. These gifts include prophecy, teaching, exhortation, word of wisdom and word of knowledge. These gifts provide contemporary contextualized interpretation of God's will (prophecy); instruction in the revealed content, attitudes and expected skills needed to function and mature as Christians (teaching); encouragement, reproof, and correction (exhortation); insight into making appropriate judgments which comply with God's will (wisdom); and clarity of understanding into what God has revealed (knowledge).

The third category of spiritual gifts provide another essential serving component. These gifts include leadership (*proistamenos*), administration (*kabernesis*), serving/helps, giving/liberality, mercy, hospitality, faith and discernment of spirits.

Leadership suggests going before, governing, directing, standing before as to protect, assisting, representing, caring for, helping, furthering, and sponsoring. The emphasis on its use in the New Testament is not one of authority, but on the efforts for the salvation and spiritual maturation of one's followers. The gift of administration presents the picture of the coordination of efforts in giving direction. The frequently-occurring gift of serving/helps is exemplified in the appointment of the seven deacons who helped with the present task or need. Some people are gifted with the constraining desire to give. Often these same generous people are enabled to have extraordinary means as well to employ their gift of liberality. Benevolence, a sense of seeking justice for the oppressed and advocacy for the distressed, characterizes the person gifted with mercy. Some receive joy from their gift of hospitality in serving and caring for others in their home for their benefit and the glory of Christ. Unusual trust, conviction, commitment and vision based on this conviction appear in the life of one gifted with faith. Often those people with this gift will exercise this gift in their prayer life with dramatic results. Christians gifted with discernment can identify what is of God and what is from Satan. Issues of spiritual warfare, demonizing and temptation clearly appear to them. They serve an important body-conscience function.

Sign gifts constitute the fourth major category of spiritual gifts. As "signs" they point to the authentication of the message and messenger, especially for nonbelievers and new believers. Among these gifts are tongues, interpretation, miracles and healings.

One important leadership-related theme becomes apparent as these spiritual gifts are studied. Paul places a strong emphasis on the functioning of individuals for the benefit of the whole church. Gifts are given for the benefit of the community of the church. Each person is expected to minister without pride and as an act of worship (Rom 12:1–3). The gifts of the Spirit are expected to be made functional through the fruit of the Spirit—especially love (1 Co 13, Gal 5:22–23). The idea of status is absent. The listing of first, apostles, second, prophets, third, teachers and then other gifts (1 Co 12:28) appears to be a chronological or sequential ranking[17] in the leadership of the church. Even with this ranking, Paul's emphasis on the mutual functioning of all of the gifts for the common good as different parts of a body is significant (1 Co 12:12–27).

The apostles were given special roles in terms of authority in the church, especially those who appeared to be the closest to Jesus—Peter, James and John—and later Paul. Their record of the gospel, their writings and teachings were all considered both by themselves and the early church to be authoritative and normative (cf. Gal 1:8–9).

Even so, they were not beyond being corrected and instructed as when Peter was censured by Paul for ethnocentrism and hypocrisy. Peter had customarily been eating with non-Jewish Christians. However, when a delegation of Jewish Christians who were sent from James in Jerusalem arrived, Peter would not eat with the non-Jewish Christians for fear of criticism from the Jewish Christians. Paul sharply criticized him for this duplicity (Gal 2:11–16).

Summary of Biblical Values

Several of the more important general values which undergird the concept of Christian leadership are summarized below. These values apply interculturally. While the specific applications and forms will vary from culture to culture, they may still serve both as guidelines for action and evaluative criteria for Christian leadership.

1) Christian leaders should function as servants. They are to be evaluated primarily by the criteria

of the servant model of leadership as lived and
taught by Jesus and his apostles as the norm for
Christian leaders.

2) Christian leaders should behave with integrity in
ways which are above reproach in their communities.

3) Christian leaders should be distributed within the
church, with different persons "leading" according to the particular gift he/she may have, e.g.,
teaching, pastoring, or showing hospitality.

4) Christian leaders should use spiritual power as
their primary power base rather than physical or
social power.

5) Christian leaders should not base their leadership
on their own rank, status or power for personal
gain.

6) Christian leaders should contribute to the purpose, fullness and functioning of the church.

7) Christian leaders should reproduce themselves
through others, by such means as contextual
preparation, discipleship, empowerment, and
legitimation.[18]

8) Christian leaders should be selected for a particular purpose based on the person's calling and
demonstrated commitment and competence.

Given these key values which apply both to the development
and functioning of Christian leaders, questions about how to
work from these values to see the development of Christian
leaders begin to emerge. The following chapter introduces some
of the basic patterns God uses to develop men and women to
become leaders. From these patterns we can identify some of the
directions in which we may take initiative in the intentional
development of others to become leaders.

End Notes

1 *Katartizo* appears in the following texts: Lu 6:40; Eph 4:11; 1 Thess 3:10; Heb 13:21; 1 Col:10; 1 Pe 5:10; Ga 6:1.

2 See K. H. Rengstorf. *"Mathetes"* in Gerhard Kittel. *Theological Dictionary of the New Testament* (trans. by Geoffrey W. Bromiley (Grand Rapids: William B. Eerdmans Publishing Company, 1967), IV:416.

3 See Rengstorf, 1967, IV:416.

4 Richard J. Foster, *Money, Sex and Power: The Challenge of the Disciplined Life* (Cambridge, MA: Harper and Row, 1985):201–207.

5 *Ibid.*

6 The writers of the New Testament use several Greek words which are translated as servant in English: *diakonos* is a servant viewed in relation to his work, so stressing his activity particularly as in the rendering of personal service when the stress is on humility and love. *Doulos* is used to focus on the relationship of the servant to his master, thus emphasizing his accountability, responsibility, obedience and undivided allegiance. *Huperetes* focuses the servant relationship on his superior, thus emphasizing the authority he is under to carry out orders. *Leitourgos* is a servant in relation to the organization that employs him, so highlighting the administration he is part of. *Therapeia* is a servant who waits upon the master to provide personal care or assistance. *Misthios* is a temporary hired servant. Jesus contrasts the hired servant with a good shepherd's concern (Jn 10:12- 13). In Mt 20:1–16 a landowner hires *(misthosasthai)* workers at different times to work. The principal point is that the reward is entirely at the discretion of the employer. *Oiketes* is a servant named for his sphere of service, that is, the household. Jesus uses this word to remind the disciples of their single source of authority and that they are members of God's household. *Pais* is a servant of the lowest status in either age or responsibility. Such a servant was not given responsibility over other people. Even though the status is low, the *pais* is still under the protection and care of the Lord (cf. Philip Greenslade. *Leadership, Greatness and Servanthood* (Minneapolis: Bethany House Publishers 1984):3 and David W. Bennett, "Images of Emergent Leaders: An Analysis of Terms Used by Jesus to Describe the Twelve" (Unpublished manuscript, March 1989).

7   John Kirkpatrick, *A Theology of Servant Leadership* (D. Miss. dissertation, Fuller Theological Seminary, 1988).

8   David W. Bennett, "Images of Emergent Leaders: An Analysis of Terms Used by Jesus to Describe the Twelve" (Unpublished manuscript, March 1989):1.

9   Walter Bauer, *A Greek-English Lexicon of the New Testament and Other Early Christian Literature* (trans. and adapted by William F. Arndt and F. Wilbur Gingrich, (Chicago: The University of Chicago Press, 1957):422.

10 Bennett, 1989:85.

11 The Greek culture was deeply affecting the eastern Mediterranean area at the time of Christ. The Greek language was widely known and Greek thought permeated the learning centers of that whole area. Several key Greek concepts which conflict in some crucial ways with Hebrew values had been accepted into the synagogue and temple leadership. The Greek approach to the use of schools and schooling which grew out of the Greek social structure deeply affected the synagogue and later the church. Whereas the Hebrew idea had been that education should be holistic, centered in and through the family and essentially religious, the Greek idea was based on schooling, hierarchy and status. These Hellenizing influences were contrary to the traditional Hebrew concepts of leadership and education (Barclay 1974). These same Greek values persist in Western society today and have often been the source of church/mission or leadership tensions, especially in non-Western societies.

The Greek concept of education was largely a one-way communicative process. Some had the information or knowledge and passed it on to others. This facet of Greek thought leads to another. Social privilege was gained through educational competition. Plato's philosopher-kings were those who had progressed furthest through this educational system. The Greeks conceived of knowledge as having its own existence as a commodity. It could be acquired. Learning was seen as reaching out for that knowledge. Knowing was seen as the basis for doing. The Greek idea related the knowing with the doing.

The Hebrew concept of knowledge, in contrast, was a close integration of knowing and doing, and learning through doing and reflection (cf. Ward 1978:14; William Barclay, *Educational Ideals in the Ancient World*, Grand Rapids: Baker Book House, 1974).

12 Ted Ward, "Facing Educational Issues," *Church Leadership Development* (Glen Ellyn, IL: Scripture Press Ministries, 1977):22.

13 See Bennett, 1989.

14 Acts 20:35; 1 Cor 4:16; 7:7; Phil 3:17; 4:9; 2 The 3:7; 2 Tim 1:13.

15 John Knox, "The Ministry in the Early Church," in H. Richard Niebuhr and Daniel D. Williams, eds. *The Ministry in Historical Perspective* (New York: Harper and Row, 1956):21.

16 Charles H. Kraft, *Christianity and Culture* (Maryknoll, NY: Orbis, 1979).

17 G. G. Findlay, "St. Paul's First Epistle to the Corinthians," in W. Robertson Nicoll, ed., *The Expositors' Greek Testament.* (Grand Rapids: William B. Eerdmans Publishing Company, 1961), 2:729–953.

18 Adapted from Edgar J. Elliston, "Biblical Criteria for Christian Leadership," *Curriculum Foundations for Leadership Education in the Samburu Christian Community* (Ph.D. Dissertation, Michigan State University, 1981):187–226.

CHAPTER FOUR

PATTERNS OF SPIRITUAL
LEADERSHIP EMERGENCE

As Pastor James and Paulo met to discuss the development of new leaders, Chun Kim and Chege Kamau, two of the younger leaders in their congregation, joined them. "Can we see any predictable ways Christian leaders develop? Do these patterns fit in multi-cultural situations like ours? Can we in fact do anything that will facilitate or enhance the development of the people God is calling into ministry? Can we understand what the Spirit does in the life of a person to bring that person into leadership?"

Understanding how spiritual leaders emerge is important both for the maturation of our own personal leadership and for our equipping others in their development.

Popular Myths

Many leadership myths continue to cloud our thinking and divert our energies. These myths disrupt both the selection processes and the development of new leaders. As with other myths, they contain enough validity to make them plausible and in some cases even useful. However, overall they do not serve us well.

We often perpetuate the Born Leaders Myth among our churches. We may even turn to scripture and look at such men as Moses, Samuel, David or others. We may say, "They were born to lead." However, without going further into this idea, let me suggest that this view is a myth. Following this myth leads us into confusion about the selection of leaders and provides no insight about how they might be developed.

The Social Development Myth continues to have prominence. Many believe that leaders simply emerge as a result of the social pressures of the time and place. Again, some biblical leaders such as Joseph, Moses, Gideon, Samson, Saul, Esther and Nehemiah are cited. Again, when we look more closely, this myth's reliability fades. It does not help in the selection or development of new leaders. Nor does it guarantee leadership effectiveness in new contexts.

The Leadership Training Myth is more tricky. It says, "We can train people to be effective leaders." If you read and believe the promotional literature about the management training seminars and workshops or the various M.B.A. programs offered around the world, you may come to believe that anyone can be "trained" to be an effective leader in any context. All a person needs is the right information, the right skills, and the proper motivation. The seminar, workshop, or college training program is guaranteed to provide all three and if you are not satisfied, you can take the seminar again!

While Christian educators may not be so crass about our advertising, in practice that is what we in Christian leadership development and, yes, theological education often say. Christian college and seminary recruiters suggest that we can make effective Christian leaders out of whomever may come.

Fred Fiedler, who has probably supervised more leadership-related research than anyone today, not long ago published an article entitled, "Leadership Training Does Not Produce Leaders."[1] Kouzes and Posner[2] further debunk this myth based on their research.

The president of a Christian college once told me that what happens in the classrooms of that institution makes little difference in terms of the effectiveness of the graduates. The key issue he sees is student selection. If the educational programs (and courses) are not flexible as is the case in most colleges, students should be selected to "fit" the programs. A given educational program will not fit every student nor will a given educational program fit all of the goals a college may have.

We should be careful then, not to be too enamored with our training programs and expect more of them than they can or will in fact produce. Be careful of this myth.

The Myth of Projection misleads many. We tend to believe that the way the Lord has dealt with us and led us through our families, friends, churches, schooling and ministries to where we are now should be normative for others.

This myth is particularly damaging as one begins to work cross-culturally. Most church leaders will face cross-cultural ministry issues in the future whether they begin their ministries in Bombay, Buenos Aires or Berkeley. Most churches will be in the growing pluralistic urban population. Urban centers are becoming increasingly pluralistic and multi-cultural. Many rural areas now are experiencing a growing pluralistic cultural mix. If your ministry is to be effective, you simply must face the issue of cross-cultural ministry. If you face that ministry projecting your own image and experience on those people who would be your followers, you may be disappointed to find they do not follow well and that their children are impossible to reach.

One of the saddest examples of this myth of projection is what is happening in many parts of the world in theological education today. Too many missionaries and the Two-Thirds World church leaders they have taught assume that Bible colleges and seminaries are *the* answer for Christian leadership development and multiplication. Unfortunately, too often the establishment of Bible colleges and seminaries marks the beginning of the decline in the growth and multiplication of the church.

I recently visited a community of churches in a central African country and the Christian college which serves to equip their leaders. When I met with the principal and faculty of this college, they proudly shared their conviction that what was needed was just like what they had learned in a Bible college in the U.S.A. They even had visiting instructors from that college teaching the same courses they taught in the U.S.A. The dress codes, texts, teaching methods, worship styles, and church leadership practices were all the same as what had been experienced in that small Midwestern American college. When I visited in the churches, neither the national leaders nor the missionaries could understand why their churches were stagnant and considered irrelevant in their community.

The myth of projection also occurs at the personal level. One tends to generalize from personal experience and suggest that others should have a similar experience. We criticize other faith communities for this projection, but fail to look closely at what we are doing.

The Myth of the Social Sciences leads us into increased relativism and debilitating syncretism. I owe a great debt to the social sciences, particularly anthropology, psychology, sociology, and education. I intend to continue to learn from these social sciences and to apply many of the insights they provide. However, many people in the social sciences deny any distinctives to the Christian faith. They would not see Christian leaders as any different from any other leaders. They would not see the elements which go into the development of spiritual leaders as any different from a political or business leader. They would describe the church simply in terms of a social organization without seeing its spiritual dimensions. We can learn much about leadership from the social sciences. We can learn much about the patterned structures of our churches and parachurch structures from the social sciences. However, I firmly believe that God has revealed some things for us and that we are to be part of the *ecclesia*, that is, God's "called-out ones."

The Information Myth deceives many of us. We tend to believe that if we know more, we will be more. If we know more, we will be more effective leaders. Jesus did not command, as some of us mistakenly read, to "teach all things." That is a serious problem many churches, Bible colleges' and seminaries' programs now face. It is a growing problem as Two-Thirds World churches are influenced by Western theological education. We strive to "teach all things" rather than "teach obedience in all things" He commanded. To know about is not to be. To describe is not to do. To list is not to apply. Information will not save us. We live in an information age where to have access and to know are key values. However, the old hymn "Trust and Obey" continues to stand against the deceit of this myth. We sometimes look disparaging at what we call "primitive" or "uncivilized" societies because of their dysfunctional and incredible myths. Perhaps we should look again at ourselves. Would we do better to know less and obey more?

Moving Beyond the Myth

If we are to understand both how spiritual leaders emerge and how we can fulfill the mandate the Lord has given us to "equip" and to "teach obedience" in all that He commanded, we must move beyond these and other similar myths.

While the development of spiritual leaders generally follows predictable patterns, it is always highly personalized by God, other leaders who share in the equipping and by the emerging leaders themselves.

Three different persons interact in a series of contexts to facilitate a person's emergence as a spiritual leader. 1) The Holy Spirit plays the key role through His empowering superintendence. 2) The emerging leaders allow the gift of faith from the Holy Spirit to be exercised through their obedience. Through their obedience the Holy Spirit opens new opportunities both for spiritual growth and ministry maturation. 3) Existing leaders become the Spirit's mouthpiece and hands for contextual preparation, ministry assignments, recognition, encouragement, legitimation, correction, empowerment and other "hands-on guidance."

Recognizing some of the complexities of leadership generally is important. Christian leadership has some essential distinctives, so it is important to look briefly into the development of these leaders. An approach to understanding this distinctive kind of leadership begins with God's revelation and then moves into our present situations.

The approach sequence I am suggesting is simple. The beginning step is a review of what the New Testament writers specifically teach about leadership. What is commanded? What is taught about leadership? What are the revealed criteria for understanding and evaluating leaders and leadership? What are the critical values which must be considered in worldview changes?

These specific New Testament teachings then serve to set the framework for interpreting the hundreds of anecdotal accounts in both the Old and New Testament. However, without a perspective which is grounded in the firm teachings about leadership, these anecdotal accounts may be interpreted to support nearly any view of leadership.

With these clear teachings in mind, one can then move to an examination of the emergence of biblical leaders—both "good" and "bad"—to see patterns in emergence, selection and transitions. The writer of Hebrews reminds us,

> Remember your leaders, who spoke the word of God to you. Consider the outcome of their way of life and imitate their faith. Jesus Christ is the same yesterday and today and forever (13:7–8).

The Scriptures record leadership information and insights about more than a hundred men and women in the Old and New Testaments. We may observe both positive and negative examples of many critical leadership concepts and principles in a variety of cultural and historical settings.

Having established our values, we may then test the social science approaches and glean many additional insights both from these disciplines and as we look at the lives of biblical leaders. Some of the insights will be positive and others will be negative.

Another stage in our inquiry is to examine the lives of contemporary leaders to learn how God is currently working. We can profit by looking at mature leaders of all five types, recognizing that the Lord calls and gifts men and women for each kind of leadership. We can expect that the Lord uses the same patterns now as He used for personal spiritual maturation and ministry or leadership maturation with the leaders described in Scriptures.

Patterns of Development and Emergence

A foundational principle for the emergence of Christian leaders is stated in Ro 8:28–30: "And we know that in all things God works for the good of those who love him, who have been called according to his purpose." God does indeed work in all things for good to those who love him and have been called according to his purpose. He works in the context both to prepare and to stimulate growth. He works through existing leaders to counsel, guide, correct, and assist. He works internally in the emerging leader in spiritual formation and ministry maturation. He works within the context, existing leaders and emerging leaders to bring the emerging leaders' giftedness, ministry roles, and status together. He seeks to bring it all together for the good of the individual, the church and His own honor, as the individual demonstrates faithful obedience.[3]

To understand the ways God works to develop a person as a leader, it is helpful to look at the whole life of the person and the ways the person responds to events, personal encounters and situations. God uses these "process items"[4] as learning experiences to develop the emerging leader. They are used throughout a person's lifetime, beginning with the formative stages through maturity.

As noted above, the Lord works in all things for the good of those who are called (cf. Ro 8:28). Believers can be assured that in every interaction and situation the Lord can and will work for their good. God uses these interactions and situations to develop character and competence. He also uses them to clarify His calling, gifting and commissioning. He provides these learning experiences to confirm his guidance, protection and vindication. He uses these learning experiences to empower the person with the necessary means to influence in the context to which he/she is called. As one experiences these learning experiences, the process of selection continues. By obediently responding to the learning experiences God provides, one is selectively guided out of some leadership ministries into others through a maturation process.

Clinton identifies three principal stages of development in the lives of spiritual leaders.[5] These developmental stages provide a framework for understanding how God interacts with a person in developing that person's relationship with Himself and as a leader. The Holy Spirit can be seen to work through a variety of commonly shared "learning experiences" or "process items" in each of these developmental stages. In each of these stages the work of the Spirit is evident as is the response of the emerging leader. An evaluation of spiritual leaders in Scripture or currently living will demonstrate many powerful lessons, not the least of which is that God remains sovereignly in control and that He seeks to work with emerging leaders for their best interests and for the good of the church.

The three principal ministry-development stages begin with a foundational stage during which the initial calling, commissioning, commitment to follow and initial training occurs. The direction for later development is shaped in this early period. The developmental focus of the second stage is the leader's competence. Character formation, value formation and skill development characterize this second major period. The transition into the third stage occurs when the focus of one's ministry shifts from flowing out of one's competence to one's character. This third period is characterized by a matching of gifts, role and stages. Typically, a leader does not enter this third stage of development until after 40–55 years of age.

Clinton divides these three stages into six periods which allows a person to see God's initiatives more clearly: Sovereign Foundations, Inner-Life Growth, Ministry Maturing, Life Maturing, Convergence and Afterglow.[6]

Sovereign Foundations

The earliest stage of God's actions to develop a person as a spiritual leader appears in the sovereign foundations which the Lord lays. In these foundations God sets the groundwork for the life of the leader. In reflection a person can often see God at work even before birth to prepare the way for a person's ministry. Circumstances, family, friends, social contacts, religious upbringing, education and/or many other variables are brought together in a sovereign way to influence the person for good and for the kind of ministry to which God is calling a person to serve. God's work in laying these foundations can often be clearly discerned in retrospect even before one's conversion. Through these foundations one may see the establishment of one's leadership potential.[7]

The appropriate response of the emerging leader to God's sovereign preparations is simply to respond affirmatively and to take advantage of the foundations the Lord has facilitated.

I was reared in a Christian family in a community that was largely Christian. My home town was "dry," that is, no alcoholic beverages were allowed to be sold there. My parents, grandparents, and great-grandparents were Christian leaders in the community where I was raised. The question of whether or not to attend church was never an issue. We would double-up on chores on Saturday with feeding the stock to be free on Sunday. In the winter we would bring out the snow-moving equipment and clear the roads on Saturday. In the summer we did not work on Sunday, even though all of the other days were long. Participation in church programs was expected, regardless of peer expectations. Our home was opened to the homeless and the abused as well as to the passing missionary. My grandparents often paid the tuition of struggling ministerial students and helped significantly with the financial needs of a nearby Christian college. Issues of ethics and justice were met head-on. My father, for example, was concerned about some community school issues, so was elected to the local school board. It seemed that money was always in short supply, yet my parents' practice of tithing allowed me to observe God's faithfulness demonstrated. My father died of cancer, yet while he was seriously ill he had a profound effect on all of the churches in the little town where we went to church, including our own fairly narrow-minded congregation, the Pentecostals, the Methodists and even the Roman Catholics. Even the secretaries in the county courthouse broke for Bible study and prayer.

In addition to my family and the church influence, the community certainly had an impact on me as well. Stability was a strong feature. I had teachers in elementary school who had been students of both my mother and grandmother. I also had teachers who had taught my mother. Through the time I graduated from high school, I only knew of one family that separated. I never knew a single divorce. Through these solid Christian foundations the Lord began to work with me.

As a leader begins to move into the transition out of this phase, the first steps of leadership are taken and the leader begins to recognize the Lord's working within.

Inner Life Growth

After conversion, one can see the Lord at work bringing spiritual life and vitality to the new believer. During this phase, essential spiritual formation occurs in which one's character is formed and one's leadership potential is at least partially identified. During this period in the life of a believer, three kinds of tests typically recur to help in the building and refining of character. Integrity checks test one's heart intent. Word checks test one's guidance from Scripture. Obedience checks test one's faithfulness in obedience.

The successful passing of these checks/tests is required for the continued development of the leader. With the successful passing of these checks, growth may be expected in the spiritual life of the emerging leader. During this stage the "emerging leader" may engage in a beginning ministry, but the focus is clearly on the spiritual formation of the person rather than the followers. During this phase the emerging leader usually receives some kind of "training" for ministry in which accountability plays a key role. This training may be informal, unstructured modeling or it may be structured in out-of-school, nonformal ways such as in an apprenticeship, conferences or seminars. Occasionally, during this phase one will enter a formal training program such as a Bible college or seminary.

Chris was converted from a nominal Catholic background. After his conversion, he began to actively seek to learn about and live the Christian life. He participated in the new members' class, men's retreats and was regular in Sunday school. As he and his wife continued to actively participate with other young families in the church, he began to grow restless. One Sunday afternoon he and his wife came to our house to complain that they did not have any ministry to do and to discuss going to Bible college. Following some discussion about ministry and growth in our local church, the two of them began working with the junior high young people. Chris began meeting on Saturday mornings with one of the elders for prayer, Bible study and reporting on his spiritual disciplines such as Scripture memory. Over the next year the junior high department grew significantly more than any other sector in the church. People began noticing Chris. He began to be asked to give devotionals. His growing spirituality has come to the attention of the whole church leadership. Church leaders began talking about his "going into the ministry." The inner life growth began to spill into ministry wherever he was.

The transition from this phase in one's development appears in a moving from receiving to giving. The transitional focus is less on the development of the leader and more on the leading. The emerging focus is more on the followers and their needs.

Ministry Maturing

In this third stage the emerging leaders begin to identify their spiritual gifts and skills for ministry. These emerging leaders are increasingly "released" to use and develop their gifts and skills in ministry. The emerging leader in this phase often moves into a ministry which becomes the prime focus of his/her life. Much of the training which is most effective in this stage of development comes from experience. The Lord works with the emerging leaders to begin teaching lessons which relate to relationships and the development of an integrated view of ministry.

During this phase the emerging leaders take steps to use and develop their gifts. As they are beginning to use their gifts, they often learn important lessons of submission and authority. Or, to put it in another way, they learn more how to be followers. During this stage they begin to catch the vision which God has for their lives. A sense of calling becomes much more clear.

After a summer internship in Caracas, Eric and Chris returned full of enthusiasm to get on with their plans for full-time mission service. Eric soon graduated from a Christian college and began graduate studies. No one could doubt Eric's call. All he talked about was the ministry to which the Lord was calling him. However, before he could go, he was to experience both disappointment and some frustration. He was expecting to "go on staff" with his home church to gain further experience with the church and to be freed from his job to devote full-time to ministry and preparations for leaving for Caracas. However, the church suffered a leadership crisis and in the ensuing transition the budget did not allow any additional staff. He was still eager to go, but was counseled that his response/reaction to the present frustration was being observed. Recognizing the authority of the leaders in the church, he redoubled his teaching ministry with young married families and sought more counsel from the church leaders. Never complaining, but rather seeking to learn what the Lord might be teaching in what he perceived as a frustrating delay, Eric's ministry maturation took new leaping strides. While still in their twenties, Eric and Chris learned how the Lord works with a person and family to develop maturity for ministry.

A strong characteristic of this phase is the active "doing" of the emerging leader. The leader's character up to this point has certainly been under development, but now a transition begins to occur in the leader's thinking. The realization comes that ministry flows out of who one is. A "doing-being" switch seems to occur in this stage.[8]

Life Maturing

During this fourth phase leaders come to realize that "mature ministry flows from a mature character."[9] A mature character develops out of the crucible of hardship, trials and difficult "spiritual processing." While many spiritual leaders may experience difficult "spiritual processing," many do not recognize the Lord's working with them for good through the situation and so miss the opportunities for growth. During this period, one's spiritual authority may increase. While the increase of spiritual authority is not a primary goal, it is a clear product of a maturing spiritual relationship with God.

To facilitate the maturation purpose, God often allows an intense time of processing in the life of the leader during this phase. In the midst of these crises, the leader often has an opportunity to reflect on the circumstances and his/her life and ministry. If the leader comes out with a renewed commitment, the Lord will continue to bless with maturation and an extended ministry. Otherwise, the leader will likely reach a growth plateau where the influence may begin to decline.

"Be patient, the Lord is not finished with me yet." My ministry in Ethiopia was a busy one with the supervision of a growing evangelism and church-planting ministry, administration of a busy clinic, linguistic research leading to the development of a literacy program, and a growing leadership-development program which had about 600 men listening to new cassette-based lessons weekly. Ethiopia was experiencing a time of political unrest, with the local feudal chiefs harassing the Christians at every opportunity and the Marxist youth campaigners stirring up dissension in the communities around us. Then I fell ill with hepatitis. For six months I was too weak to even walk the fifty meters from my house to my office. It was a time of acute frustration, anger at my weakness and depression.

After recovering and apparently not learning the lessons the Lord would have taught had I been more willing, we began to face another crisis of isolation. The Marxists had successfully stirred up enough trouble at a nearby mission station that we had to evacuate the missionaries and close all of the programs, including the school and clinic. In the ensuing riots two colleagues and I were nearly killed twice, but escaped because of the Lord's interventions. Then came the decision to reopen Tosse. My wife, Donna, and I were asked to move from our busy productive ministry to reopen that station. The Marxists had infiltrated the church and had caused serious local problems. Isolation was pressed upon us as Christian friends were beaten, their homes burned, and they were often detained because of contact with us. Through the course of the next year, when we were threatened at gunpoint several times, experienced the indignity of an illegal search of our home, being taken hostage and being harassed by the police and in the local government offices, the Lord was continuing to teach us lessons about His faithfulness and our need to trust Him. Lessons about prayer and the urgency to equip local leaders began to be more deeply impressed on me during this period.

During this phase one may increasingly experience an awareness of the converging of one's giftedness and one's role(s). As this awareness grows, the leader moves into the next major leadership-development phase.

Convergence

As the Lord works with a leader, He provides spiritual gifts and then works to bring the leader's gifts, statuses and roles together. As one's gifts, statuses and roles converge, the maximal effectiveness of one's ministry is realized. The leader's response to the Lord's leading during this stage is one of trusting and making decisions which lead to a convergence of role and giftedness. One may experience this coming together of giftedness and present level of maturity at deepening levels through one's life. However, in maturity the Lord seeks to bring it all together.

Doug is a gifted preacher and teacher. He also has a deep commitment to the Oromo people. He has developed an understanding of their culture and is sensitive to Oromo cultural issues. However, since a serious throat ailment, he can not preach regularly. And, the Ethiopian government forced him and his wife to leave Ethiopia following the revolution. Still deeply committed to the Oromo people, he began producing Oromo radio broadcasts to be aired over the Far Eastern Broadcasting Association from the Seychelles into Ethiopia. At first the response was meager, now after several years, the Oromo church depends on the regular, consistent, encouraging Bible teaching which comes from Doug. Regular listeners number about 600,000—many times what he could have done in the country. His gifts of teaching, exhortation and encouragement have come together within this very significant radio ministry.

Afterglow

Some leaders due to age or infirmity move out of their experience of convergence of giftedness and role. During this phase of their life they bring honor to God for His faithfulness. They bring encouragement to other leaders in their declining sphere of influence.

Bob had a distinguished ministry as the senior pastor in a large urban church. From that church countless young people entered full-time ministries both in the U.S. and in missions in a number of denominations. The church was known as a giving church. Following his outstanding ministry there, he joined the faculty of a large seminary where his warm pastoral spirit brought a new spiritual freshness on campus. No longer did students just learn *about* what it meant to be Christian, they had an outstanding model who expected it of them. After retirement, the faculty of the seminary, recognizing his deep spirituality and contribution to the faculty, asked him to come back as the chaplain to the faculty. Honored by having an endowed chair of evangelism named for him, he remains a humble servant whose lifetime of ministry is an encouragement to the younger faculty members who are in their forties, fifties, and sixties. His spiritual authority runs deep.

Major Spiritual Learning Experiences

The Lord provides an appropriate set of processes or learning experiences in each subsequent developmental stage. These processes build on and emerge from the basic developmental processes the Lord uses from the outset. The Holy Spirit continues to work through circumstances, other people (both Christians and non-Christians), existing leaders and the emerging leaders themselves to bring about the developmental processing needed to mature the leaders toward Christlikeness and for ministry.

Curricular Characteristics of
Spiritual Development

The Lord is indeed *the* Master Teacher. When one reflects back over a lifetime of the Lord's leading, three characteristics may be seen through the hundreds of learning experiences or "process items" He has used in the life of a person to specifically develop that person to be the kind of leader He wants him/her to be.

Continuity

The first of these characteristics is continuity. The Lord has a lifelong "program" of equipping and development available for a person in that "walk." He continues to reiterate and reinforce basic lessons which may have been learned even in childhood. For example, the Lord continues to develop a leader through processes related to prayer.

Jephthah was a leader steeped in crisis whom the Lord used as a crisis leader. Daniel's faithfulness in small things, such as eating, praying and giving credit to the Lord, served him well in spite of repeated tests as he served the world's most powerful kings of his day.

Sequence

Another characteristic of the Lord's instruction is sequence. The lessons He teaches increase in difficulty and significance. The new believer is not ready for the bringing together of giftedness and role through isolation testing or conflict, and the mature believer generally does not face the same basic integrity checks so needed by the newly emerging leader.

Barnabas's opportunities for service were met with faithfulness and, as he was faithful, ministry opportunities grew. Beginning in Jerusalem, then being sent to Antioch, the difficulties of his tasks increased, as did their significance. Remaining faithful and employing the growing number of gifts, Barnabas saw his sphere of influence grow from the Jerusalem church to Antioch, Cyprus, into what is now Turkey and in the lives of the apostle Paul and John Mark.

Integration

The third characteristic of the Lord's equipping is its integration. It all fits together. The gifts, call, the wide range of learning experiences—both positive and negative—all work together for the leader's good and for the good of the kingdom if the leader will give himself/herself to the Lord.[10]

The Lord provides a wide range of learning experiences individually designed for the emerging leader's instruction. How the emerging leaders respond to the learning experiences will determine their rate of development and the leadership development stages to which they will attain. The Lord remains sovereign, however, in terms of the gifts and the type of leader one will become. Mature leadership does not necessarily mean a top management or administrative role. God calls many to be mature Type I leaders who serve with small groups and are seldom known outside of their own small locale or local church.

Ralph Tyler provides insight from curriculum theory which helps us understand some of what the Lord does with the learning experiences related to "process items." He defines a "learning experience" as "the interaction between the learner and the external conditions in the environment to which he can react."[11]

He goes on to say, "Learning takes place through the *active behavior* of the student; it is what *he* does that he learns not what the teacher does.[12] The Lord provides a continuing stream of "process items," which may serve as learning experiences if one responds to them as such.

Learning Principles in Spiritual Leadership Development

Tyler suggests five principles which further help us understand what the Lord does in His lifelong instructional processing. Each of these principles applies to what the Lord does with us.

Appropriate Practice

For a given objective to be attained, the emerging leaders must have the experiences that give them opportunities to practice the kind of ministry behavior which is desired.[13] Thus, we see leaders beginning with small ministry tasks which, while helpful to others, provide opportunities for practice and personal spiritual and ministry growth.

Satisfaction

The learning experiences must be such that the student obtains satisfactions from carrying on the kind of behavior implied by the objectives.[14] When one looks at the ways the Lord leads, one can see that He leads to peace, a sense of fulfillment and joy. While life may at times be difficult, the Lord leads beyond the pain and suffering.

Contextually Appropriate

The experiences should be appropriate to the emerging leaders' present attainments, their predispositions, and the context in which they are likely to function in applying the learning.[15] The learning experiences the Lord uses are like the teaching in an old single-room country school in which students were aware of what others in other grades were learning, but they had learning experiences specifically shaped for them, given their present levels of development.

Multiple Options

Even as many particular experiences can be used to attain the same educational objectives, so also the Lord works through many different kinds of experiences, situations and relationships to accomplish His purposes.[16]

Multiple Outcomes

Just as the same learning experience will usually bring about several outcomes, so also a given process item may facilitate the learning of several spiritual truths or the learning of a truth at multiple levels. The same experience, relationship or situation may produce a very different outcome in the life of another person because of the person's individual response to that learning experience. One must then be aware of the possible negative outcomes as well as the positive ones.[17]

Summary

Spiritual leadership emerges as the *Spirit* works through both men and women in their accepting faith and committed obedience. Spiritual leadership development, then, is a Spirit-led and intentional process. It is a lifelong process which requires both the faithful and discerning obedience of the existing leaders and the emerging leaders. God has called us to serve—to serve Him. In serving Him we influence others—we lead. God has called us to lead by serving and then to serve by leading.

This chapter has outlined some of the patterns of activities God through his Spirit works in the development of a person. The following chapter extends this view by looking at the role of the Holy Spirit in the development of leaders from a different perspective. This perspective lays the base for our entering into the leadership development equation.

End Notes

1   Fred Fiedler, "The Trouble with Leadership Training is that it Doesn't Train Leaders," in William R. Lassey and Richard R. Fernandez, *Leadership and Social Change* (La Jolla, CA: University Associates, 1976):238–246.

2   James M. Kouzes and Barry Z. Posner, *The Leadership Challenge How to Get Extraordinary Things Done in Organizations* (San Francisco: Jossey-Bass Publishers, 1987).

3   Clinton has done ground-breaking research in the area of Christian or spiritual leadership emergence patterns. He began his research with a study of biblical leadership and biblical leaders. His research is further based on the personal descriptions of leadership emergence among about four hundred Christian leaders. These men and women represent both mature leaders of Types III, IV and V who have had significant missiological commitments. They have served in about fifty different nations of the world. About ten percent of them were women. They range as leaders from leaders of small groups in a local church to international denominational and parachurch senior executives. He has written several pieces about this process and several character studies of biblical characters such as Barnabas, Joseph and others.

He has looked at the emergence of leaders from a developmental perspective which parallels the stages in human development in developmental psychology.

Some of these resources include *Leadership Emergence Patterns Manual*. Altadena, CA: Barnabas Resources, 1986; *The Making of a Leader*. Colorado Springs: NavPress, 1988; *Leadership Emergence Theory*. Altadena, CA: Barnabas Resources, 1989; "Leadership Emergence Patterns," *Theology News and Notes*, June 1989.

4   "Items in the course of daily life which God uses in a special to 'process' a leader toward development"—J. Robert Clinton, "The Emerging Leader," *Theology News and Notes*, June 1989:25.

He provides a more technical definition in another context: "those providential events, people, circumstances, special interventions, inner-life lessons, and/or anything which God uses in the leadership development of a person to indicate leadership capacity (inner integrity, influence potential), expand that potential capacity, confirm appointment to a role/responsibility which uses that leadership capacity [and/or] direct the leader along to God's appointed ministry level for the realized potential" Clinton 1987:56.

5 Clinton, 1989.

6 J. Robert Clinton, *The Making of a Leader.* Colorado Springs: NavPress, 1988)

7 Joseph was not fully aware of how or why God was working with him until the famine in Egypt (Genesis 45:3–11). Similarly, while Moses identified with the Hebrews and opposed their oppression in his early manhood, he apparently was unaware of the Lord's preparations in his life when he encountered the Burning Bush (Exodus 3, 4). Barnabas, however, very clearly prepared the way for Saul in Jerusalem with Saul's full knowledge.

8 See Clinton, 1987:176

9 Clinton, 1988:6:3.

10 See Ralph Tyler (*Basic Principles of Curriculum and Instruction.* Chicago: University of Chicago Press, 1950:55) for a more complete treatment of the issues of continuity, sequence and integration.

11 Tyler, 1950:41.

12 Tyler, 1950:41.

13 Tyler, 1950:42.

14 Tyler, 1950:43.

15 Tyler, 1950:43.

16 Tyler, 1950:43.

17 Tyler, 1950:43–44.

CHAPTER FIVE

THE SPIRIT'S ROLE IN LEADERSHIP DEVELOPMENT

> *Paulo challenged Pastor James, "I am convinced the development of Christian leaders should be different from what I do at my business. But, how should we approach their development? What is to be done? Who should do what? I want to get going with this project. I am ready to start . . . Just give me the word!"*
>
> *Pastor James replied, "Maybe we should pray first . . .?"*

The Holy Spirit plays the key role in the development of leaders. However, to understand the overseeing and dynamically interactive part He plays, the overall picture must be brought into focus.

Leadership Development—An Overview

Leadership development is by no means a hopeless task. In spite of the complexities of leadership noted in the first chapter and the myths which confuse the church, the Lord is very much involved in the process. And, we as leaders are expected by the Lord to actively participate in the process as a major part of our calling. The mandate comes from the Lord as a part of the Great

Commission in the "teaching of obedience." The apostle Paul leaves no doubt when he said,

> It was he who gave some to be apostles, some to be prophets, some to be evangelists, and some to be pastors and teachers, to *prepare* God's people for works of service, so that the body of Christ may be built up until we all reach unity in the faith and in the knowledge of the Son of God and become mature, attaining to the whole measure of the fullness of Christ (Eph 4:11–13) (Emphasis added).

The apostle Paul further emphasized the issue in his second letter to Timothy (2 Ti 2:2) where he committed to Timothy the task of entrusting what he had learned to faithful men who would teach others also. He repeatedly demonstrated the importance of this expectation of leaders in his own ministry. One can see this emphasis demonstrated in Paul's ministries with Timothy, Titus and the Ephesian elders, to mention only a few examples.

If one looks at the whole leadership development process, the active developmental role of the Holy Spirit appears. The ways both the existing and the newly-emerging leaders can and should cooperate with Him in this process also emerge.

I have an apple tree in my back yard. It has helped me to think about Christian leadership development. Six or seven years ago, a local nursery owner decided that it was time to plant some apple seeds. A worker began working to prepare to plant these trees. He prepared planters with potting soil. He then selected the seed and planted the seed in these planters. He cared for the young plants as they emerged. In due course some were selected for grafting. After grafting and the initial pruning, they were given time to recover and to begin growing again.

The nursery worker continued to watch these plants and it was not long before they were transplanted. The trees continued to be cultivated, watered and watched for parasites and disease. Care was given to the context in which they were to grow.

One Saturday morning, I went to the nursery and bought one of these trees. The tree by then was about four feet tall and planted in a five-gallon bucket. I took it home. There I prepared the place where it would be transplanted by digging a large hole, placing fertilizer in it and shaping a mound for its roots. I transplanted it and then watered it. I watched it grow with only occasional cultivation, watering and application of insecticides. Now about five years after having planted that apple tree, my family is watching a fourth batch of apples develop on that tree.

You may be asking, "What does this story of an apple tree have to do with church leadership?"

Review with me the stages of growth in the apple tree and some of the things which were done either to or for it. From these activities we may draw some parallels with spiritual leadership development.

Each of the steps along the way suggest leadership development parallels. Allow me now only to mention some of the events in the life of a tree and some possible leadership parallels.

Often when we think of developing leaders, our minds immediately turn to focus on the training of men and women to serve. However, I want us to back away for a somewhat broader perspective of leadership development. Training is important, but it is only one of many critical elements in the emergence of a leader. Leadership development involves a leader or leaders with their character, competencies and commitments. However, leadership development also involves followers with their motivations, abilities and relationships. The leadership influence process takes place in a situation of time, place and social interaction. It occurs in a framework of shared values. The development of leadership requires more than just training because training may not adequately take into account the followers, time, context and shared values.

Furthermore, the development of leaders often brings the leaders-in-training into focus without a close examination of at least two other critical roles. We often pay only passing lip service to the role of the Holy Spirit in the development of Christian leaders. We may fail to recognize that the Sovereign God whom we serve seeks to work in all circumstances for one's good, that is, a person's growth and development, and for the church. We dare not neglect nor deny the Holy Spirit's role if we are to

Horticultural Functions in Leadership Development
TABLE FOUR

Preparing the Soil	Preparing the leadership context
Selecting the seed	Initial selection of the potential leaders
Planting the seed	Initial ministry/work assignment
Cultivation	Initial protection and encouragement
Grafting	Introduction of spiritual gifts
Pruning	Disciplined growth shaping, cutting away of unproductive growth, stimulation of fruit-bearing potential
Transplanting	Moving the emerging leader to a context for additional growth or fruit bearing
Continued cultivation	Facilitation of growth
Fertilizing	Education for growth and fruit-bearing (Note parallels in purpose, timing, content, delivery system, soil condition, maturity level, cost, resources, etc.)
Fruitbearing	Reproductive transitions

to participate in the development of Christian leaders for mature ministries. Likewise, the role of other leaders in an emerging leader's development must not be overlooked or neglected.

Three basic, but very different, critical interactive roles therefore contribute to the intentional development of emerging spiritual leaders: 1) the superintending role of the Holy Spirit, 2) the selecting/equipping role of the existing leaders and church family[1] and 3) the trusting/obedient role of the emerging leader. These complementary and essential roles all contribute to the emergence of new leaders. When any one is neglected or discounted, the whole leadership development process suffers.

The Holy Spirit's initializing and integrating role is a crucial part of every stage of the leadership development process—selection, equipping, maturing, transitions, working through a person to equip others, bringing first a sense of destiny and then a sense of fulfillment as one's giftedness and role converge. He works in the context and the people in that context, through the already existing leaders and in the emerging leader to facilitate, motivate, correct and to enable the new leader to grow and reproduce. The Holy Spirit fills the most critical role throughout the whole process.

Contextual Preparation

After David was anointed to be the future king of Israel, God obviously prepared the context in which he could learn to be king. Was it coincidence that David moved from the pastoral hillside to the royal court in King Saul's presence where he could learn the inner workings of the court and character of Saul (1 Sa 16:14–23)? Was it a coincidence that Jesse sent David to see his brothers just as Goliath was challenging Israel's army (1 Sa 17:17–58)? Was it a coincidence that David's integrity before Saul was repeatedly tested even to the point of having an opportunity to kill Saul in the midst of Saul's murderous opposition and when he, David, knew he had been anointed to be the future king? (1 Sa 24:1–22) Not at all! God works in the context to provide opportunities for growth and testing for each person.

The Lord teaches through the context and circumstances. He may work subtly or very openly in the context to facilitate the emerging leader's development. Callahan writes,

> "People learn leadership best in a leadership environment wherein certain qualities are actively present ... The best environment for leadership development includes these features: objectives, authority, decision-making, continuity, competency compassion, [and] local development ... In a sense, these

qualities are the soil in which persons mature toward their leadership competencies. The "richer" the soil, the more likely that . . . [context will produce] excellent leaders.[2] God in fact provides contexts for the emergence of leaders that supplies all of these qualities.

Selection

While not many will experience the dramatic and unmistakable call that Saul had on the way to Damascus, the Spirit's call to leaders continues no less today. Leaders continue to testify of it today not only for professional and paid roles in the church, but for the many essential nonprofessional[3] and paraprofessional[4] ministries in the church as well.

In the congregation I know Sue testifies how the Lord has given her both a "burden" and "desire" as well as a vision of what she could do to help provide food for hungry people in our community. God called Peter, a former alcoholic, to lead an effective counseling and evangelistic ministry among alcoholics and their families. Dave, an engineer, lays awake nights thinking of new ways to improve the effectiveness of the lay witness ministry he leads.[5] Jim affirms how the Lord has made him increasingly sensitive to the benevolence needs in the community. Ruth testifies how many years ago the Lord called her to serve in the teaching of children. She has effectively equipped scores of others to work effectively with children over the past two decades.[6] John attests about how the Lord is continually reinforcing His call to him to plant new churches in an urban Latin culture both from within himself and from within the church.[7] And so the testimonies continue as to how God continues to call/select men and women to lead in ministry.

The Lord selects a person for a specific ministry. Among other things He matches the person with the task, followers and situation. He sovereignly selects the person who can be gifted and equipped for the ministry at hand.

Gifting—Empowering

The Holy Spirit says, "I WANT YOU!" As the Great Recruiter, He not only calls, He provides the equipment for the job. The unmerited favors He gives enables each believer to serve with effectiveness. The gifts of the Spirit (1 Co 12, Rom 12, Eph 4) aim at the good of others in the context of the church and for their equipping for service. These gifts provide the initial and ongoing empowerment of the Holy Spirit for ministry. They are the Holy Spirit's authorization to use spiritual power for God's purpose in the church. They may be seen as part of the Spirit's legitimation of His selection process.

The debate where "natural talents" and "spiritual gifts" begin and end misses the point that God is both Creator and Re-creator (2 Co 5:17). He is responsible for both. Gifting is like a fruit-bearing graft on an apple tree. The graft is a "gift" to the tree to become its fruit-bearing structure. The grafted part soon feeds the roots while the roots nourish and support it. It is indistinguishable from the tree. It becomes the tree. However, the graft is implanted into a compatible root stalk. Both the nature of the roots and the graft come from God.

In following the analogy, grafting generally occurs early in the life of a tree. However, if the owner decides later to do additional grafting, that too is possible.

The gifting is under the sovereign control of the Spirit. He decides both which gifts to give and when they are to be received. The gifts that are provided are certainly for the purpose of building the whole church, but they contribute to the individual's growth as well. The whole church will experience organic or infrastructural growth as the gifts are employed. It will also experience a deepening of spiritual growth. As these two kinds of growth emerge, the extension growth can be expected to soon follow.

Equipping

The Holy Spirit is responsible for the equipping of men and women for ministry. He superintends the whole process. It is He who works to have them thoroughly fit for ministry.

Paul wrote Timothy,

> All scripture is God-breathed and is useful for teaching, rebuking, correcting and training in righteousness so that the man of God may be thoroughly equipped for every good work (2 Ti 3:16–17).

Regardless of one's developmental stage, the Scriptures provide both the contents and the standards for "teaching, rebuking, correcting and training in righteousness." In every case the aim is for the disciple to be "complete," "mature" or "perfect" or "thoroughly equipped" for ministry.

"Word processing" expresses what the old gospel preacher did in interpreting and applying the Scriptures as having facts to be believed, promises to be enjoyed, commands to be obeyed and warnings to be heeded. The Holy Spirit continues to convict of sin, righteousness and judgment as one reads and meditates on the word (Jn 16:7–11). His ministry of drawing people to Christ is evident to all who meditate on His word.

Processing the facts, promises, commands and warnings in one's own context enables one to know, to become and to do what the Spirit would have in a given time and place. The Spirit leads in this processing both to bring about personal spiritual maturity and to facilitate the formation of one's ministry. Whether one is a Muslim student leader in the University of Djakarta, a senior-age-grade leader among the pastoral Masai of Kenya or the owner of a thriving recording business in Buenos Aires, the Holy Spirit works through the Word both to convert and equip a person to become a spiritual leader. The Muslim leader was not only converted, but led his own family and many other Muslims to acknowledge Jesus as God's Son and their Lord. As the senior-age-grade leader listened to the "Words of God," he led men and women from every village among his tribal section to faith in Christ. Following the direction he received from Scripture and the Holy Spirit, the Argentine executive has become one of the key leaders in the largest church in Latin America.

Leading Through Others

The Holy Spirit works through existing leaders to develop others. While the Spirit spoke to Cornelius, He led Peter to do the needed personal counseling and instruction (Ac 10:1–48). While commissioned by the Holy Spirit, Paul spoke personally to encourage the development of men like Timothy and Titus (1 and 2 Ti and Tit). He worked personally through Paul with a wife-and-husband team, Priscilla and Aquilla (Ac 18:2,26; Rom 16:3; 2 Ti 4:19). Paul wrote words of encouragement under the Spirit's direction for Philemon (Phoebe, Rom 16:1–2; Onesimus, Phil). Again, under the direction of the Holy Spirit Paul wrote to bring correction in the lives of the people quarreling in Philippi (that they were apparently quarreling in Philippi can be seen in Phil 2:1–4,14; 4:2–3), the ones who were divided over factions, spiritual gifts, moral issues and other significant problems in Corinth (1 Co).

The Holy Spirit works through leaders to correct other leaders. He worked through Peter to correct some of the early racial prejudice of the Jewish Christians (1 Co) and then later through Paul to bring correction in Peter's ministry for his remaining prejudice (Gal 2:11–13). Paul through the guidance of the Holy Spirit sent others on ministry assignments, for example, Timothy and Titus (cf. ministry assignments of Timothy: Ac 16:3, 17:14, 19:22, 20:4; 1 Co 4:17 and Tit 1:4, 5).

The Spirit works through existing leaders to prepare the situation, select, equip and discipline the development of "emerging" leaders. As He leads through existing leaders, He continues to "develop" them.

Growth Processing

The Holy Spirit continues to direct the development process in emerging leaders through several complementary ways such as interaction with the Word, through existing leaders, contextual events and internal reflection. The Spirit even works for one's good in circumstances which one might describe as "negative" such as conflict, life-threatening circumstances, isolation, persecution and the like. He provides both instructional and reflective guidance. Each process, however, can be checked for both validity and reliability with the primary source He has provided in the Scriptures. Some of the other general developmental means both illustrated in Scripture and experienced today include the leading of other spiritual leaders, the "internal" witness of the Spirit and contextual opportunities and events.[8]

Some of the growth-processing activities of the Holy Spirit can be understood in terms of the horticultural process of pruning. Pruning is "the removal of part of a plant for the benefit of all the plant. Pruning has three basic effects: it directs growth, it improves health, and it increases production."[9] When understood from a horticultural perspective, pruning is a useful cyclical process. It can help "rejuvenate an old, sparse shrub or tree."[10]

When a leader makes a transition from one role or status to another, the Holy Spirit may initiate "pruning" in the life of the leader to insure health in the new situation. The Holy Spirit may also use the "pruning" process to correct or repair damage. As with a tree, pruning may help insure health by removing diseased or irreparably injured parts. As with a wise gardener, the Holy Spirit oversees this process. People, as plants, vary widely in their need for pruning. Some seldom if ever need pruning; others need it regularly. The Holy Spirit decides, as a wise gardener on the basis of the kind of plant, the context and His purpose for the plant.[11]

Several leadership parallels are analogous to pruning. Most leaders, to be optimally effective, need occasional, recurring correction to optimize their fruit-bearing potential. Their "growth" may overtax their fruit-bearing potential or it may be inappropriate for the situation they are in. The reproving correction will not likely be for gross errors or defects, but for shaping and fine-tuning their fruit-bearing potential. Normally, heavy pruning occurs only where there has been serious damage or neglect.

Pruning is never done as deliberate punishment to a tree. It is always done to improve health, direct growth or increase production. Similarly, the normal discipline of a leader is not aimed at punishment, but rather at improved spiritual health, growth in effectiveness and an increase in fruitfulness as desired by the Lord in his/her situation.

Peter was one whose recurring correction served in these ways. Jesus reproved him on more than one occasion, yet he remained an outstanding leader among the apostles. Later, after leading the church in its reaching across ethnic barriers (Acts 10), he still needed some correction for his racial prejudice. The apostle Paul provided this pruning function. This disciplinary pruning as initiated by the Holy Spirit may come through convicting insight from studying God's Word (1 Timothy 2:15–16). It may be pressed on a person through integrity or obedience tests. Crises and negative experiences may serve a refining purpose. Occasionally, criticism may serve a useful disciplinary function. Often the wise interventional counsel by other believers serves to bring discipline in the life of both the emerging and more mature leader.

Pruning not only affects the individual, but the context in which the individual lives as well.

> Pruning to direct growth is also a way to control the microclimate of your garden. The cuts you make can affect the movement of air, the degree of sunlight and shade entering a yard, air temperature—even the condition of the soil.[12]

When applied to the church leaders, the local congregation will certainly be affected. Clinton describes[13] how God works through a wide variety of "process items" to facilitate and stimulate both spiritual and ministry development. Ministry and leadership clearly emerge out of the Spirit's inner working. The trust, conviction, commitment and confidence in God which provide the bases for a solid influence all emerge out of the Spirit's work within a person. These maturing and leadership qualities all emerge as the person responds to the word, opportunities for obedience and the tests which check his/her integrity and intentions. The Holy Spirit "delegates" authority or that right to influence to leaders to lead. This delegated authority contributes directly to the emergence of a person as a leader. As one matures spiritually, spiritual authority appears.

A follower's allocation of authority to a spiritual leader and his recognition of a leader's spiritual authority emerges from the recognition of God's working in and through the life of the leader to influence others for their good toward God's purposes. This "delegated" and "allocated" spiritual authority is not based on one's own status or power. Rather than emerging out of such commonly expected forms of power as expertise, information, organizational connections, personal charisma, or control of rewards and punishments, it flows out of a committed servant-hood (Mt 23:1–12).

Superintendence

Spiritual leadership development is a key role of the Holy Spirit. The Spirit is the one who gives the overall supervision. He superintends, empowers, equips, gifts, guides, directs, provides insight and delegates the authority to lead. It is *His* work. However, the Holy Spirit has chosen to require two other crucial roles in the developmental process. These roles supply crucial elements to spiritual leadership development. Without these roles new leaders will not emerge. The roles of the existing leader and the role of the emerging leader both facilitate the process under the Spirit's superintendence. However, the Spirit still provides the key guidance for both the existing leader to lead and develop new leaders and for the emerging leader to become all that he/she can be. Each of these two roles needs to be examined in the light of what the Holy Spirit does in leadership development. The next two chapters seek to address these two roles from that perspective.

End Notes

1   Existing leaders may well be family members and people in the community as well as people in the church who deliberately seek to influence the emergent leader.

2   Kenneth L. Callahan, *Effective Church Leadership: Building on the
Twelve Keys* (New York: Harper and Row, 1990):152.

3   Nonprofessional leaders are classified as "Type I" leaders.

4   Paraprofessional leaders are classified as "Type II" leaders.

5   Sue, Peter, Dave, Jim would all be considered as "Type I" leaders.

6   Ruth is a good example of a "Type II" leader whose influence reaches
beyond her own small group.

7   John would be a "Type III" leader now because he works full time in
this ministry and has had specialized training.

8   See J. Robert Clinton. *The Making of a Leader*. Colorado Springs:
Navpress, 1988.

9   Charles Deaton and Michael MacCaskey *All About Pruning*. San
Francisco: Ortho Books, 1978:7.

10   Deaton and MacCaskey, 1978:7.

11   Deaton and MacCaskey, 1978:7.

12   Deaton and MacCaskey, 1978:7.

13   Clinton, 1984 and 1987.

CHAPTER SIX

THE EXISTING LEADERS' ROLE IN LEADERSHIP DEVELOPMENT

> *Paulo again turned to Pastor James, "Now I see the development of Christian leaders is the work of the Holy Spirit. We can live in expectation and hope because of what the Spirit is doing. But, surely I am expected to do something. What should I do to help my friends, Chun Kim and Chege Kamau to become the kinds of leaders they believe God is calling them to be?"*

As the Spirit works through existing leaders, He seeks to develop them even as emerging leaders are developed. The Holy Spirit works through existing leaders to facilitate the emergence and development of new leaders. These leaders fit into every type. One should not expect another person to emerge as a leader by simply coming under the influence of one other leader. Leaders emerge and are developed in a community where many different people will have varying degrees of influence on the emergent leaders. As a person begins to emerge as a leader, his/her status and role sets will shift as will the status and role sets of the other "leaders" who influence him/her.

Even as gardeners facilitate the growth and development of a fruit tree, existing leaders facilitate the growth of a new leader. Gardeners do not grow for the tree nor can they make it grow. They simply work to create the conditions in which the Creator can bring the nature of the tree to full fruition.

Gardeners listen to the owner's instructions and then prepare the soil, plant the seed, care for and cultivate the seedling, prune, fertilize, transplant and harvest as directed. Similarly, existing leaders demonstrate parallel roles to equip God's people for works of ministry (Eph 4:11–13).

As a gardener works with a variety of plants which are at various stages of development, existing leaders also work with a variety of followers whose maturity and developmental stages differ. Wise leaders still discern and respond appropriately to these differences.

The nursery staff of the nursery near my home has a wide diversity in terms of competency and influence. The absent owner sends policy directives and guidance. However, within the local staff are people with degrees in horticulture. They know all of the technical names and information to care for any plant they have. Competencies range downward to the water-boys who simply water where, when and how much they are told. However, the whole staff works together for the good of the plants and their growth.

Whether one is a trained theologian isolated from direct ministry or a small group leader, every Christian leader has as a part of his/her leadership portfolio the development of others for ministry. It is not just the task of the theologian, college professor, or pastor. The responsibility rests squarely on the shoulders of every Christian leader.

The responsibility is not singular for any one individual existing leader. No single person is called or expected to do everything needed in the development of another person to be a leader. Rather, the Christian community, and in particular the whole distributed leadership, is responsible for a wide variety of leadership-development functions which primarily mirror the complex work of the Holy Spirit.

Obedient Discernment

Even as a gardening staff for a nursery must understand the owner's desires for their work of preparing the soil, planting and other activities, so the existing leaders in a congregation must obediently discern God's will for leadership development. Leadership development is the work of the Spirit. The Spirit gives the gifts of apostle, prophet, evangelist, pastor and teacher to "equip," "teach," "mature," "complete," "perfect" others for the work of ministry. Within the body of Christ, one primary leadership task is knowing the God-given purpose, goals and objectives for that body. The purposes, goals, and objectives will be consistent with what is revealed in Scripture. The basic instructions about what leaders ought to know, be and do are in the Word. When leaders are committed to carry out these instructions, then they can cooperate in the task of leadership development.

Where does one begin the process of leadership development? Leadership always has three basic requirements: a leader, follower(s) and a situation. These elements are as essential to leadership as oxygen, fuel and heat are to fire. If any one is removed, leadership will disappear—the fire will go out.

Existing leaders are expected to be discerning in at least three ways to facilitate the development of new leaders. Obviously, the first ongoing, required discernment is of God's will and guidance for the situation at hand. The Holy Spirit provides guidance through the Word, the church and through other means the existing leaders have already learned. Certainly, Bible study, prayer and other spiritual disciplines serve to keep their discernment sensitivities attuned. Spiritual guidance is clearly culturally conditioned in terms of the forms it takes. However, it will always remain consistent with the clearly revealed Word of God. Whether through such diverse guidance forms as "double confirmation" in which multiple independent witnesses or circumstances attest to the same guidance, visions and dreams which are often less-accepted forms of guidance in the West, or through new applicational insights gained in the study of God's Word, God through His Spirit seeks to meet the need of existing leaders for obedient discernment of His will. To be able to discern the Spirit's leading one must have a strong personal relationship with the Spirit.

Existing leaders must be careful not to just inject their own personal or private perception of what God's will is for another person. The Spirit works consistently and so what is clearly revealed in the Scriptures, confirmed by the Christian community and discerned by the existing leaders should be taken into account. Leaders do speak for, represent and participate in the Christian communities they lead. Their role is not just personal.[1]

The second kind of discernment relates to the emerging leader—the present leader's disciple. Many issues require discernment to assure appropriate leadership and developmental direction. The disciple's goals, calling and giftedness, ability or capacity for the task at hand, his/her commitment, level of motivation and character are only a sampling of the issues requiring discernment. To know or discern any one of these issues requires a personal relationship with one's disciple. To presume one can begin to develop another without this discernment will very likely lead to disappointment.

Discerning the emerging leader's spiritual maturation level, giftedness, calling, and commitment all require time and a personal relationship. This discernment is unlikely to be accurate without having been supported by prayer and the guidance the Spirit gives to the existing leader.

The third kind of discernment relates to the situation in which the leader and disciple serve. The existing leaders must discern the relevant aspects of the situation which will bear on the leadership transactions and the development of their disciples. From the situation one should discern such issues as values and external constraints for either ill or good. The disciple should certainly be matched with the situation where both the disciple/emerging leader and his/her followers will benefit.

Such was undoubtedly the discernment of the apostle Paul when he sent Timothy to Thessalonica and Titus to Crete. It was not just a question of availability, but a discerning match of giftedness in the situations. Why did the apostles send Barnabas to Antioch? Because they recognized the match of a bilingual-bicultural Christian Cypriot whose gifts matched the situation.

He understood the cultural and gospel issues. He was gifted in encouragement and linking.

One critical role of existing leaders, then, is to discern God's will, the emerging leader's condition and the situation to care for the new leader, his/her followers and their situation until the emerging "leader" can lead on her/his own. One may need to provide more heat, oxygen or fuel to get the fire going. The existing leaders may have to give more attention to the leader, the followers or the context to facilitate the process of development.

Existing leaders require flexibility to be effective in carrying out their roles in the development of new leaders. This flexibility relates to several interactive issues. Both the motivation and ability of the emerging leaders vary over time as they both relate to the ministry at hand. Time, task structure, size, group structure and history of the group involved, relationships among the group members and resources all come into the existing leaders' attention and should affect their leadership-style choice.

To facilitate the required discernment, one important responsibility of leaders is to pray for their followers. Every step along the way should be based on prayer. Jesus prayed before the selection of His disciples. He prayed for those who would later become His disciples and then for their disciples. The apostle Paul wrote of his specific prayers to his disciples. Supporting one's disciples in prayer and working through prayer to discern the Lord's will and leading is an important part of one's leadership. Samuel demonstrated the importance of prayer even in the midst of a serious leadership crisis and transition. Even when the people had rebelliously insisted on having a king when Samuel would likely have been angry with the people, he prayed for them and promised to continue to pray for them (1 Sam 12:1–25, esp. 23).

By looking at only two prayers one can see the breadth of the issues one may include in praying for one's followers. In Jesus' prayer in John 17 we see a number of issues to include in prayer: 1) protection for unity, v. 11; 2) joy, v. 13; 3) protection from the evil one, v. 15; 4) sanctification by the truth, v. 17; 5) for their followers unity, v. 20; 6) for their followers' closeness to God so that others may also believe, v. 21; 7) for their followers' unity, v. 22; 7) for all followers to be present with the Lord, v. 24 and 8) that both the Father's and Jesus' love may be in them, v. 25. The focus of the prayer is not on effective management, but on the quality of one's life.

The apostle Paul explains his prayer for his disciples in Colossae (Co 1:9), illustrating his concern for them and providing a model for us. He continually prayed, "asking God to fill you with the knowledge of His will through all spiritual wisdom and understanding." Paul and Timothy prayed this prayer so that their followers in Colossae might live a life worthy of the Lord, and may please God in every way by bearing fruit, growing in knowledge of God, being strengthened with power for endurance and patience and by giving thanks (cf. 1:10–12). Again we see a focus on the followers' quality of life as well as on "bearing fruit." In addition to other leadership functions, leaders lead by praying. Secular writers note that leaders represent their followers. In Scripture this representation suggests an ongoing priestly intercession before God.

Selection

One important role of the Holy Spirit is the selection of leaders. Existing leaders carry out their complementary "selective" role for existing leaders in new leader discovery and recruitment. The discovery of the men and women the Lord has  chosen requires discerning observation of faithful men and women. Effective recruitment requires a knowledge of what leadership or ministry needs exist in the congregation and existing leaders of every type and every level also need to acknowledge all the members of the congregation and their present abilities and potential abilities to fill these needs. Both the discovery and recruitment processes are made effective by prayer.

The selection of leaders continues as a critical issue whether one is selecting another to be a village evangelist, a Sunday school teacher, an elder, a pastor, a district superintendent or a national chairperson. Selecting the right person for training is no less important. The selection of the leaders probably has as much impact on the final outcomes of a task as any other combination of variables.

How can one validly and reliably select the right person for the task at hand? Stogdill's list of traits[2] provides clues about the characteristics of the person. A person's adherence to a shared worldview and value base is also critical. One's "task maturity" should also play a part in the selection process. Hersey and Blanchard suggest that "task maturity" consists of competence and motivation as they relate to a particular task.[3] The selection of people for spiritual leadership also requires an assessment of the person's spiritual and ministry maturity as they relate to the ministry/task at hand.

Some of the interrelated but essential variables one should consider in the selection process include the following: one's spiritual gifts or gift mix, technical competence, motivation, spiritual maturity, ministry maturity, one's demonstrated faithfulness in carrying out responsibilities, the task or ministry to be done along with its structure and priority, the support community where the leader will be assigned, the followers along with their interrelatedness and relationship with the leader, the available power the leader has, both personal and corporate, and the shared value base. While effective selection occurs in many different contexts, the risks and complexities remain evident to every person who has ever tried to select another person either to lead or to be developed as a leader.

Existing leaders should know the local situation and the emerging leaders well. By knowing both the situation with its needs and the emerging leaders with their capabilities the existing leaders should be able to help with the selection process in matching the emerging leaders and the situation. By knowing both the new leaders and the situation, the "older" leaders may be able to encourage both the followers and the emerging leaders together.

Certainly, a key role of existing leaders is discernment. They must discern the Spirit's leading, the congregational/community needs and discernment *and* the level of development of the emerging leader. As the new leaders emerge, the existing leaders must recognize their development so it may be encouraged, empowered and employed. Their discerning recognition occurs in the dynamic leadership situation where the emerging leaders' faithfulness and influence are observed over time and with the people who are being influenced.

Michael Youssef supports these two simple trustworthy principles: 1) People may not recognize their own leadership abilities until someone discovers them and gives them opportunities. 2) People emerge into leadership positions when they know they are wanted.[4]

The very process of selection contributes to the emergence of leaders because of what social psychologists call the Pygmalion Effect. The Pygmalion Effect is based on a Greek myth about Pygmalion. Pygmalion sculpted a statue of a beautiful woman. He fell in love with the statue and through the power of his love and expectations he brought the statue to life.[5] The expectations of leaders on people who respect them have a powerful molding effect for good or ill. Expectations shape the perceptions of others and influence one's behavior toward them. Expectations often become self-fulfilling prophecies. If we expect others to excel, they are likely to excel. If, however, we expect them to fail, they will unfortunately probably not disappoint us.

Selection on the part of existing leaders requires a careful discernment of the Lord's leading. An arbitrary selection of whomever for whatever leadership role is open will only bring disaster for the group and for the person who would have become a leader in another context. One's giftedness, motivation, present level of ability or competence and sense of calling all require careful, selective discernment on the part of the existing leaders.

One may be gifted as a teacher and called to serve among junior high young people. For the existing leaders to discern the teaching gift and miss the calling by assigning the person to teach adults would invite frustration and disappointment to all concerned.

The selection function of existing leaders must discerningly follow the leading and actions of the Holy Spirit in selection.

Preparing the Context

As a part of the situation, existing leaders already have an influential role in the situation. They have the key responsibility, then, to prepare the situation for the emergence of the new leader. The better prepared the situation is the potential for the initial healthy development of a new leader.

Ideally, the initial ministry environment into which the "emerging" leader is planted will be characterized by a strong sense of mission, not just activities or busyness. This sense of mission will provide the initial nurturing for intentional directionality that anticipates the future and moves toward the future. It will be an environment where the emergent leader is delegated the right to do what is to be done, not just given a task to do. Kenneth L. Callahan says, "the greater the range of [delegated] authority, the more likely the level of leadership competencies is to grow. The more fully persons are given authority, the more likely they are to develop their leadership competencies."[6] And, "it is decisively crucial to provide persons with an authority range that, at a base minimum, is commensurate with their current competencies."[7]

The context should be structured so that decision-making is modeled in a participatory way in accomplishing significant objectives. The environment should be characterized as "coaching" or encouraging, not a "correcting" or legalistic context.

As a gardener prepares the context for the new plants, so existing leaders prepare the situation for the new leader. The emerging "leader" must be given legitimate space to grow into having influence. The existing leaders must be careful not to overshadow and stifle the emerging "leader," but build his/her credibility and legitimacy. The legitimacy can be established by showing why the emerging leader has "the right" to influence or lead in that situation. Establishing the legitimacy of the new leader establishes his or her authority both from "above" as the followers see that authority or the right to influence is being delegated to him or her by the community. As existing leaders reflect the work of the Holy Spirit, a part of their work is to confirm the emerging leader's spiritual gifts and their appropriateness for the emerging leader's present ministry assignment. When the existing leaders address the recognition of legitimacy among the followers, the "allocated" dimension of authority or the giving of the right to be influenced is established.

Gardeners choose and prepare the place so the texture, fertility, acidity, moisture and temperature of the soil are all appropriate for the young plant. Similarly, more mature leaders prepare and clarify the role, relationships, and status for the new leader not only with the new leader, but with his/her "followers" in the situation. The more mature leaders assure the presence of the necessary support services, encouragement, structure information, supplies and equipment. They structure the tasks and roles to effectively utilize the personnel and other resources. The existing leaders prepare the context by addressing both the group's interpersonal relations and work-related relations for both cohesiveness and teamwork. They monitor and facilitate appropriate leader-follower relations. They prepare the context so it will stimulate growth, not just tolerate it. They prepare the followers for collaboration, that is, their laboring together.

The contextual preparation is always done with the purpose of the church in mind to bring all peoples to Christ and then to bring them up to responsible discipleship. Contextual preparation *always* moves beyond mere involvement.

Additionally, in preparing the structural elements of context the existing leaders should give attention to issues of consideration. Existing leaders can greatly facilitate the establishment of the support networks for the emerging leaders.

The preparation of the context requires the same attention whether one is involved with a new believer and his/her first ministry or a more mature leader who moves into a new context. When preparing contexts for ministry or leadership development, attention must be given to the variety of contexts needed to stimulate development of *all* of the needed ministries in the church.

John the Baptist prepared the way for Jesus (John 1:6–13; 19–34). Barnabas prepared the way for Paul in the Jerusalem church (Acts 9:27). Paul prepared the way for Onesimus with Philemon (Philemon). Jesus prepared the way for Philip in Samaria by interactions with local people, including the woman at the well (John 4:7–26) as well as miracles of healing.

In preparing the situation, existing leaders set the process of a leadership transition in motion. Changes in influence begin to be anticipated. The emergent leader can seldom fulfill this role, because the existing situation is seldom immediately conducive to the planting, growth or transplanting of a newcomer.

Possible initial growth situations are as wide as the ministries of a church. One may work with a Sunday school teacher to open a place for a junior high assistant. The person operating the sound system may prepare a role for someone to assist. An elder may be asked to "apprentice" a faithful Sunday School teacher to expand the eldership. The senior pastor may equip an associate who will become the senior pastor of a new congregation or succeed him. The organist may teach another to serve in that role. Every leader's role is to prepare each ministry to be an equipping link to the next generation of leaders not only for the local church, but for new churches. No place exists for "dead end links" in the church.

Preparing the Initial Followers

The kind of leader the emerging leader is becoming will determine what followers the existing leaders need to prepare. The basic principle is to prepare the people who are expected to be within his/her initial sphere of influence. The first task is to clarify the ascribed status of the emerging leader in the ministry context with the initial followers. The establishment of the emerging leader's assigned position in the group is an important function of the existing leader. Not only do the existing leaders address the question of status, they must also address the issue of the expected role for that status. What is that newly-emerging leader expected to do in his or her new position? Leaders should clarify the followers' expectations for the appropriate level of direct or indirect ministry. Will the new leader interact with them and influence them on a face-to-face basis or indirectly through other people? Will he/she influence only two or three or indirectly influence the whole community through organizational policy-making? The existing leader has the task to prepare the initial expectations of the followers for the new leader.

When Richard recruits a new teacher for an adult Bible study group, part of his role is to prepare the group for the acceptance of the new teacher. Simply sending the new teacher to an unsuspecting group is not adequate. A transitional preparation is needed. Existing leaders can best do that.

Initial Ministry Assignment

After preparing the soil, gardeners plant the seed expecting it to take root and grow. Existing spiritual leaders similarly place the emergent leader in a prepared ministry context expecting his/her growth.

Gardeners transplant the young plants in suitable places which match their requirements for sunlight, temperature, moisture and acidity. Similarly, if effective leadership is expected, the emergent leader must be placed in a suitable growth environment. Fiedler suggests three things by which the situation can be judged for suitability for the leader: 1) task structure, 2) leader-follower relations and 3) the power given to the leader.[8] Several illustrations of the appropriateness of ministry assignments which take these variables into account may be drawn from the assignments the Jerusalem church gave Barnabas or the ministry assignments Paul gave to Timothy and Titus.

The parallel role to legitimation among the followers must also be done with the emerging leaders. Even as legitimation establishes the right of the emerging leader to lead among the followers, the initial ministry assignment or leadership committal serves to establish the person in the new status and role relationships. The new status and accompanying role(s) are committed to or entrusted to the emerging leader (cf. 2 Tim 2:2). The newly emerging leader is given a trust for which he or she is to be accountable and which is expected to "benefit" the One for whom the trust is held. The basic value of servanthood runs deeply through every ministry assignment because the assignment is never to be given or accepted for personal gain (1 Pet 5:1–4; 2 Ki 5:15–27).

Initial ministry assignments are always done with hope, faith and expectation. The more clearly the expectations are communicated to the emerging leader, the greater the potential for this realization. Expectations by someone who is respected have a powerful motivating effect. The motivational effect can be multiplied not only by this personal acceptance of the emerging leader, but also by this repeated public affirmation. For example, as Karen accepted the role as director of the children's summer camp program, Dorothy outlined her expectations of the program and for Karen's personal growth. Seeking to please Dorothy and to do a good job with the children, Karen began to work hard. In teachers' and other leaders' meetings Dorothy made it a point to commend Karen on her planning and to speak of her high expectations. She was not surprised when Karen, her staff and the young people all exceeded her expectations.

If the person is not yet a leader, then the most appropriate ministry assignment will be a task which will both test the faithfulness of the person and provide satisfaction in its successful completion. The status should reflect the person's spiritual maturity and the accompanying role should be within the person's range of motivation and ability. Generally, an initial status and the accompanying roles will not carry a high level of visibility. In addition to fitting the maturity of the emerging leader, it should also fit the expectations of the initial followers. For early effectiveness which stimulates further growth, the expectations of the leader, emerging leader and followers should correspond as much as possible.[9]

Often, initial ministry tasks will be physical or manual jobs. The principle follows Jesus' statement in Luke 16:10 about granting increased responsibility on the basis of faithfulness in small things. Three other principles also may prove to be helpful: 1) Provide ministry opportunities which allow one to stretch, that is, provide ministry opportunities which require growth. 2) Allow the emerging leader to take more responsibility before he/she asks for it. 3) Always give the authority to do what needs to be done in the assignment. Youssef asserts, "Leadership emerges when people receive opportunities to develop themselves . . . [And,] most leaders learn on the job."[10]

Initial ministry assignment should follow close on the heels of conversion. Faithful obedience in small things contributes both to spiritual and ministry formation. "Passive," "unattached" "uncommitted" believers risk being stunted in their spiritual formation and ministry maturity. Assigning busywork just to be involved with no attendant empowering will guarantee passive, uncommitted followers whose leadership potential will remain untouched.

"Volunteerism" as it is widely known and depended upon in the church today was not the only nor perhaps the primary way of leader-ministry assignments in the early church. Barnabas was assigned or commissioned to go to Antioch. Barnabas went to Tarsus to find Saul and bring him back to Antioch to enter the teaching ministry there. The team was selected from the Antioch church to go to Cyprus. Yes, people had to be willing, but they were also called and commissioned. Ministry assignment continued to be an important part of the ministry/leadership development of the early church.

Ministry assignment continues as an important role of the existing leaders. Ministry assignment will be followed by the recognition of trustworthy service and the subsequent enlargement of responsibility or the transfer to another place for continued growth. While initial ministry assignment is crucial to allow development, similar principles apply for later assignment or reassignment.

The initial ministry assignment requires existing leaders to match the people and the ministry on the bases of the variables which promise the best possible. fit. Normally, it only takes a brief interview to assess which ministry in the church a new person will initially fit. At that point natural talents, developed skills and a person's desire to serve ought to be considered in the assignment. For example, a new member or someone who recently joined the church where I am a member who works as a sound engineer was assigned to the ministry which operates and maintains all of our sound equipment. The evidence of giftedness may then appear in that ministry. Often the gift will fit the ministry role. Frequently, however, the giftedness will extend beyond that initial ministry. One must not assume, however, that the ministry assignment must follow one's professional role.

The existing leaders place emerging leaders in a ministry context which matches the temperament, ability and motivation of the emerging leader. They are placed for *success* and growth, not frustration and failure. The situation into which the new leaders go must be considered in terms of its favorableness toward the new leader. Favorableness relates to "the degree to which the situation enables the leader to exert his influence over his group."[11] Three important variables condition the favorableness of the situation toward the leader: 1) the personal relationships between the leader and members of the group, 2) the degree of structure in the task the group has to do and 3) the power and authority the leader has in the group to carry out the task at hand.[12]

Also, the leaders must keep in mind that the emerging leaders are volunteers. Their vitality is profoundly influenced by the attitudes and feelings of the "older" church leaders. As they are assigned, existing leaders must keep the emerging leaders' constraints in mind. They have only a limited amount of time. They are not paid staff members. They are likely to make only temporary commitments to a given role until after they have attained a certain level of maturity. Even as they mature the amount of time the emerging leaders can invest may be limited. The responsibility or ministry then given to the emerging leader should not be so heavy that it will stunt one's growth and discourage the emerging leader. Rather, it should stimulate and encourage growth.[13]

Empowerment

The ministry assignments given to an emerging leader should be seen in the context of empowerment. Empowerment has three key dimensions: delegated, allocated and internal/confirmational. Each dimension directly contributes to the development of the new leader.

The delegated dimension of empowerment for new leaders comes first from the Holy Spirit and then through the existing leaders. The Holy Spirit empowers, that is, delegates the right to use His power to influence in a variety of ways which are described in Scripture as spiritual gifts. The emerging leader is granted the authority—the right—to use the Spirit's power in evangelism, teaching, liberality, encouragement or in many other ways. Spiritual power forms the primary power base upon which spiritual leaders influence other people. One develops these gifts through their use in ministry and in the context of the fruit of the Spirit.

Existing leaders again mirror the work of the Holy Spirit empowering the new leaders by delegating authority to them to lead—to influence toward God's purposes. Empowerment is the process of enabling, equipping and allowing them to make a significant contribution in a situation and then recognizing that contribution. Since power, including spiritual power, is not a fixed commodity, but an expandable potential, the empowerment of new leaders not only releases their potential for influence, but it increases the existing leaders' potential for influence with the new leaders. The more that is given, the more that remains. On the other hand, the more spiritual power is grasped, the less it becomes. Empowerment must also be seen in terms of the primary relationships one has as a leader which both empower and through which one influences. The Christian leader's primary relationship is with God through Jesus Christ so the existing leader's primary task is to build on this relationship to establish spiritual authority. The second key kind of relationship is interpersonal relationships through which "personal" power is established. Again the existing leader should facilitate and assist in building the skills for and the building of these relationships. The third set of relationships come from the emerging leader's relationship with the social structure which gives him/her status and the authority to influence on its behalf. Once again the existing leader is called to help in the building of these "personal" relationships with the social institution whether it is the church, an agency or some other social institution.

When the leader shares power with other people, those people in turn feel more strongly attached to the leader and more committed to effectively carry out their duties and responsibilities: they feel that a failure to carry out tasks lets themselves down, as well as the boss.[14]

When you strengthen others, your level of influence with them is increased. When you go out of your way on behalf of others, you build up credit with them—credit that may be drawn upon when extraordinary efforts are required. Leaders create a sense of covenant when they help others to grow and develop. When the leader is viewed as helpful, other people will more likely be committed to the leader and the organization's goals.[15] The process of empowerment contributes to higher satisfaction with one's work and is positively correlated with increased effective performance.

The third dimension of empowerment comes from the allocation of the right to be influenced by the followers. Authority or the right to use power does not just come from above, but is recognized and allocated to a leader from his/her followers.

The empowerment of spiritual leaders flows, then, from the Holy Spirit's working in the newly emerging leader and existing leaders to bring His influence to bear in the situation and followers. Look, for example, at what happened with Saul of Tarsus as he was influenced by Barnabas at Antioch and in Cyprus. It is no accident that the process of empowerment is often greatly facilitated by leaders with the gift of exhortation or encouragement. Empowering others requires working beside them without holding them back. It is the process of turning followers into leaders. Leaders are always power-brokers, but they must be power-brokers on behalf of the people they lead, empowering them and employing their power/influence on their behalf.

Three kinds of power are available for Christian leaders. Each kind must be used appropriately and in harmony with the others for one to lead effectively as a Christian. The misuse of any kind of available power will lead to dysfunctions among the followers and the loss of effectiveness and possible discrediting of the leader. The appropriate use of power will not only lead to the effectiveness of the leader, but also to the multiplication of other leaders and their empowerment. Part of the task of the existing leader is to work with the emerging leader to develop both these three kinds of power and the value base out of which they will be used appropriately.

A major part of the ministry of existing leaders is instruction about the use of power and then to participate in the process of empowerment. The power is not theirs personally to give, rather they serve as power brokers in each of the kinds of empowerment. The process of leadership development is essentially the process of empowerment. It goes well beyond training. Training is important, but leaders are not made by training nor by educational programs. Leaders may, however, be developed, equipped and empowered. One primary responsibility that existing leaders have is the development of empowered leaders.

Leadership is always based on relationships. Secular leadership writers describe personal and positional relationships which form an emerging leaders "social" power bases. Christian leadership, however, is always based on the leader's relationships with God, with others and with the social structures within which he/she leads. Christian leaders derive and develop their "power bases" from these **three** sets of relationships. It is in the context of these three sets of relationships that a Christian leader's power is legitimized. And, it is through these three sets of relationships that the Christian leader's influence is exercised.

The primary form of power available to Christian leaders is spiritual power. We seek to understand "spiritual" power through theology. Spiritual power has its ultimate source in God. Spiritual power is often demonstrated in spiritual gifts, blessings, and cursings. It is evident in a person's life in the fruit of the Spirit. Spiritual power is developed through one's relationship with God. Spiritual power is often under-developed in Western Christian leaders because of a common deficiency in the Western ("Enlightened") worldview. Social power is commonly divided into two primary categories: positional power—based on one's relationship to an organization as seen in his/her organizational status. A second kind of social power based on interpersonal relationships is often called "personal power." The social sciences have developed many means both to understand and to employ social power.

The patterned use of social power forms the base of what people generally think of in leadership styles. Christian leaders often act as though they believe that it provides all of the significant bases for their influence potential with other people. Social power or the potential for influence through sociological or cultural forms does indeed form the base for much of the influence of Christian leaders.

Contemporary management writers have further categorized these two categories of power. Christian leaders have both of these kinds of power available and will use a combination of these kinds of power in their daily leadership behaviors. However, Christian leaders should not exclude or grasp any of these kinds of power until learning the biblical values which provide both the prescriptions and proscriptions on their use.

A. **Coercive power**—the potential to use physical force.
B. **Connection power**—the potential connectedness or networking potential for influence.
C. **Legitimate power**—the potential for influence based on one's status in the group, organization or community.
D. **Reward power**—the potential for influence based on one's perceived control of rewards (financial, socioemotional).
E. **Referent power**—the potential for influence based on one's personal relationships and personal charisma.
F. **Informational power**—the potential for influence based on the information one is perceived to have.

G. **Expert power**—the potential for influence one has based on his/her perceived knowledge or skills.[16]

Position power is often based on fear. It relates to one's status in a social organization such as the church.

Personal power is based on interrelationships with the person and is described in current literature as referent, information, expertise and "charisma." Relationships based on who we are, what we know, and what we can do undergird this personal power base for Christian leaders.

Three attributes of power are not evenly distributed among different kinds of leader. They do not typically increase proportionally with different types of leaders (as from Type I to Type V). The social power available to each type of leader typically has a unique set of characteristics. For example, as extensiveness increases, intensity and comprehensiveness typically decrease. When one looks at the attributes of power and how it is distributed, an existing leader will probably become increasingly convinced of the importance of the equipping of a multitude of small group leaders in a church.

But these two social power bases, however attractive or appealing they may be, are both seductively inadequate and inappropriate for Christian leaders. Without the addition of spiritual power they are inappropriate and inadequate to accomplish the mission to which God has called us both as individuals in our families, small groups, or in the church. The reason is simple—the task to which Christian leaders are called is a spiritual task not simply a social one.

Social power provides a broad set of potential ways of influencing for good—or ill. In our ministries Christian leaders will employ various kinds of social power to influence others. However, social power is seriously limited in terms of its potential for influence in achieving Kingdom-related goals. As long as one does not touch on spiritual matters (which in fact are very few) in a way which disturbs our Enemy, a leader can use social-based power. However, whenever leaders treat issues that have any spiritual implications, they will see that social power must be linked with spiritual power to be effective.

The primary kind of power Christian leaders are to use, then, is spiritual power. It too is based on a relationship—relationship with God. Spiritual power is critically important for "spiritual" leaders to use because it is their primary power base.

The task to which spiritual leaders have committed themselves is a spiritual task—not just a physical or social one. It may involve both physical and social elements, but the task is primarily a spiritual one. The apostle Paul describes it as a "wrestling" against spiritual forces, not people. Thus, the issues are not primarily social or cultural, but spiritual.

When reviewing leadership situations through the Scriptural accounts, two levels of activity may be observed and are often explicitly presented—namely, the surface physical/social level and the spiritual level.

Spiritual power may be seen from two perspectives: 1) Power from God who is the primary source of power and unlimited in His power. Spiritual power from God is creative and builds relationships toward eternal life. 2) Power from Satan who limits and counterfeits the power of God. Satanic power is destructive, deceptive, disruptive, damaging, discrediting, isolative, selfish, lacking in self-control, impatient, accusatory, lacking in hope and lacking in joy. It leads to strife, jealousy, envy, fractiousness, chaos, death, destruction and ultimate alienation.

Satan is able to "empower" people. However, his power counterfeits God's power and only leads to destruction. Satan—the prince of this world, usurper and counterfeit—attacks through spiritual power. He attacks at every level of relationship—personal, domestic and congregational relational life. He may also use his power through physical or social means such as sickness, bondage, torment. He works to damage every kind of relationship, inner-personal, inter-personal, family, congregational, community, regional, national and international structures as well. He often uses physical or mechanical means to frustrate us such as the weather or machinery.

Spiritual power from God may be seen in people. Every follower of Jesus Christ may be empowered by the Holy Spirit to do the works Jesus did. The marks or characteristics of this empowerment to lead or influence other people distinguish

Christians from others who may use other kinds of power. The apostle Paul's description of the fruit of the Spirit provides the key set of distinctives for identifying people who are spiritually empowered.

Richard Foster writes,

> There is a power that comes through spiritual gifts, and there is a power that comes through spiritual positioning. The two work in unison. Submission gives us spiritual positioning. We are positioned under the leadership of Christ and under the authority of others. We find others in the Christian Fellowship who can further us in the things of God. We submit to Scripture to learn more perfectly the ways of God with human beings. We submit to the Holy Spirit to learning the meaning of obedience. We submit to the life of faith in order to understand the difference between human power and divine power.[17]

Spiritual power influences both the physical and social domains. Look at Jesus' healings, changing water to wine and addressing the storm. Jesus promised: "Truly, truly, I say to you, he who believes in me will also do the works that I do; and greater works than these will he do, because I go to the Father" (John 14:12). He also promised his disciples: "But you shall receive power when the Holy Spirit has come upon you; and you shall be my witnesses in Jerusalem and in all Judea and Samaria and to the end of the earth" (Acts 1:8).

However, existing leaders must provide warnings about the misuse of some kinds of spiritual power. Christians are prohibited from using forms of spiritual power which would have their source in Satan, e.g., divination, curses, engaging in satanic rituals, witchcraft, the occult, necromancy, and magic.

The employment of spiritual power is related to spiritual authority which is the right to use spiritual power. Spiritual authority is built, as is other authority, on the basis of relationship. Relationship with God emerges on the basis of two primary issues: 1) Faith (trust, conviction, commitment, confidence) and 2) Obedience. Spiritual authority like other forms of authority is both "delegated" and "allocated." God "delegates" the right to use spiritual power in part in the forms of spiritual gifts. It is accessible through prayer, praise, fasting and meditation. Christian leaders have the right to use it in intercession, or blessing. The effects of spiritual power are seen in the effects it has internally in terms of the fruit of the Spirit and externally in the lives of others as they are influenced to believe the truth, be freed from the effects of sin and as they pledge allegiance to Jesus as Lord.

God sovereignly delegates spiritual power through the Holy Spirit so 1) we can "stand" (Eph 6:12-18), 2) we can "disciple all the nations" (Mt 28:18-20), 3) we can "bind" and "loose" using the keys that Jesus promised Peter in establishing the church. The doors/gates of hell can not prevail.

Spiritual authority is "allocated" or "recognized" by other people and spirits. Spiritual authority is allocated by the people who are willing to be influenced, that is, it is recognized and allowed. Spiritual authority may be legitimized privately as we develop our personal relationship with the Lord. It may also be legitimized in public ceremonies such as "ordination" and the "laying on of hands." A person's spiritual authority is recognized in the spiritual realm. Jesus said, "Whenever two or three of you agree about anything . . . it will be done" (Mt 18:19). James writes that when elders (who have spiritual authority) pray, results can be expected (Jas 5:17). People who are demonized are led to freedom by confronting the evil spirits and taking away their bases for influencing a person by people who use spiritual authority granted by the Lord through His Spirit.

God has a plan for personal spiritual empowerment. Spiritual power may be increased by praise, prayer, fasting, meditation, study of His Word, obedience in little things/ministries, suffering for His name's sake, faithful stewardship of what has been committed into one's care, fellowship, exercising one's giftedness, rituals such as baptism, observance of the Lord's Supper, ordination, public prayer, public blessings, and instruction.

God's plan for the spiritual empowerment of others requires the obedience and participation of existing leaders. Existing leaders must continue to realize that they are not the primary power holders; they are but the conduits through whom God works to empower others. Spiritual power may be increased in the lives of others in many ways: Instruction, facilitation of spiritual formation, i.e., the building of a personal relationship with God through personal spiritual disciplines, blessing, intercessory prayer and ordination. It may be increased by appropriate ministry assignments with the authority to act, discretion to decide, public recognition of the work done.

First and foremost the job of existing leaders is to empower men and women for leadership. That in its most direct terms means the building of three sets of inter-connected relationships including: 1) legitimate relationships with the people who would be led, 2) with the social organizations in which the emerging leaders are to lead, and 3) with God through Jesus Christ whose power they are to employ. In each case two relational issues emerge: trustworthiness and competence. Both church-based equipping programs and Christian higher education have institutionalized the question of competence around sets of information and skills. The arena of competence somewhat so that even more interpersonal and organizational skills are included in the equipping of existing leaders. Existing Christian leaders have often assumed that spiritual formation, growth in Christ-likeness or spiritual and ministry maturation would automatically result from studying the Bible, theology or ministry courses. Some success can be seen. However, the more emerging leaders coming from broken or troubled backgrounds and from a less churched society direct attention is required. The issues of basic spiritual disciplines, initial ministry assignments, accountability, obedience, building trust, and the building of basic competencies must once again be considered on the agenda of emerging leaders.

When leading others in the process of spiritual empowerment, Jack Hayford offers some wise suggestions to the existing leader in a church or an educational institution who would seek to participate in the spiritual empowerment of emerging leaders:

   a. You must be credible and practical not mystical or peculiar.

   b. You must be scriptural, systematic and sensitive, not
      subjective, sporadic or mocking.
   c. You must be patient, instructive and understanding, not
      demanding, dictatorial or presuming.
   d. You must be human and touchable, acknowledging your
      own doubts and difficulties, but bold and aggressive,
      moving forward with conviction.[18]

Three kinds of encounters or confrontational issues using
spiritual power need to be taught to emerging leaders.[19] Existing
leaders generally begin with a truth encounter which aims at
understanding. It forms the base for an allegiance or commitment encounter which is required for a person's salvation.
However, some people are not able to deal with the issue of
truth until God's power has been demonstrated. This kind of
demonstration or encounter is often called a "power encounter"
in which that which is under Satan's power is taken from him. It
may be demonstrated in any number of ways such as healings,
deliverance from demonization, signs, wonders and miracles.
The result is an emotional freedom to exercise the mind in a truth
encounter so that the will may engage in an encounter of allegiance. Power encounters which do not lead to a commitment to
Jesus Christ as Lord are ultimately not useful. We should continue as we have in the past to warn people about being overly
interested in these kinds of phenomena. However, on the other
side of the picture, we should be careful not to deny what God is
obviously doing as well. Existing leaders are expected to assist
in the development of the emerging leader's relationship with
God so that his/her spiritual authority allows the use of spiritual
power in these three ways.
   The employment of spiritual power is primarily for the
purpose of waging spiritual warfare. Again, Jack Hayford
addressed the scope of this warfare in ways which are instructive for the existing leader:

   a. Dealing with personal, domestic and congregational
      attacks.
   b. Ministering deliverance from sickness, bondage and
      torment.

   c. Intercessory prayer in persistent ways for local, regional and international issues.

   d. Steadfastness under persecution in suffering or through martyrdom.

   e. Witnessing by testimony, proclamation or service in a hostile environment.[20]

Existing Christian leaders have the task both to instruct in the use of power and then to participate in God's empowering men and women for ministry. Empowerment requires the establishing of three critical relationships—with God, with others, and with the social organization(s) in which the emerging leaders serve. The beginning point is a focus on spiritual formation with help to develop personal growth relationships with God through Christ.

Existing leaders will help emerging leaders establish "win-win" agreements and structures both with individuals and the social systems in which they will lead. They will take responsibility to help establish helpful structures and systems which allow for the emerging leader to develop a "response-ability." Existing leaders will continue by helping them to establish and practice "self-supervision" in a spirit of high accountability.

Visionary and transformational leaders can not be "trained," but they can be developed as existing leaders are willing to build expectations, hope, trustworthiness and competence in the emerging leaders. They can be developed as existing leaders assist in the development of the key empowering relationships with God, others and with the organization.

Rosabeth Moss Kanter suggests four ways to empower others in the realm of social power. These four principles apply to the ministry assignments of emerging leaders:

1. Give people important work to do on critical issues.
2. Give people discretion and autonomy over their tasks and resources.
3. Give visibility to others and provide recognition for their efforts.

4. Build relationships for others, connecting them with powerful people and finding them sponsors and mentors.[21]

One empowering role of existing leaders mirrors the work of the Holy Spirit. While the Holy Spirit provides the gifting and spiritual authority, the existing leaders facilitate its implementation. Existing leaders *authorize* and legitimate the new or emerging leaders in this status and these role relationships. The initial forms of power (especially referent, legitimate, connection, information and expertise) may be in the hands of the existing leaders. However, a critical part of their role is to transfer these kinds of potential for influence to the emerging leader or build the kind of institution and personal relationships for and with the emerging leader which will legitimately supply these kinds of power. Their role includes empowerment.

Existing leaders also serve a key role in the spiritual empowerment. Existing leaders are expected to continue from the beginning through retirement to serve as priests to intercede in prayer for the emerging leaders. They should also empower the emerging leaders through both private and public blessings. They are expected to serve as models to emulate. Existing leaders then can serve to facilitate the spiritual empowerment process by standing with/bearing with the emergent leader as he/she learns to praise, pray, meditate, fast, wait, study the Word, suffer, and serve accountably.

The power source is the Holy Spirit, so existing leaders serve in the process by introducing the emergent leader to the Holy Spirit.

Just as one empowers another socially by the steps outlined above, one aids in empowering spiritually by similar steps. First is the introduction to the legitimizing source of power and then one is placed in situations where that power is expected to be responsibly used.

Empowerment is accomplished by public rituals of transfer, private encouragement and personal disengagement which allows the engagement of the new leader in ministry. Empowerment may also be facilitated by and in the building of specific power bases. An existing leader can aid in building spiritual authority by a continuing discipleship relationship focusing on spiritual and ministry growth processing. Information, expertise, referent and connection power can all be developed through an ongoing mentoring-sponsoring relationship. Empowerment through mentoring leads then to another important role of existing leaders, that is, equipping.

Equipping

One recurring role of a gardener is the application of fertilizer. Gardeners take care to apply the right kind of fertilizer, the proper amount at the best time in a way the plants can best use it. They apply it with a specific purpose in mind. They select which plants are to receive it. The cost-benefit ratio is critical to the gardeners. They pay attention to the amount, knowing that too little or too much may threaten the plant. They also consider the plant maturity, soil conditions and climate. Similarly, the existing leaders' teaching or equipping role requires care. They know that the context, amount, timing and delivery system for the instruction are crucial. They also consider the new leader's maturity as well as the followers and situation. Without continuing care, the wrong instruction can be ill-delivered in a damaging amount at an inappropriate time to potential leaders.

Delivery System

The appropriate instruction of emerging leaders requires a contextually-sensitive delivery system. Combinations of three basic delivery systems are normally used for the development of leaders. However, the balance among them varies widely from one type of leader to another.

Informal education provides the most important and continuous means of delivery for instruction. It is unplanned and relational. It is sometimes called enculturation and occurs for every person in all social situations. Informal education provides one's worldview and entry into all of his/her cultural forms.

Nonformal education is planned, out-of-school instruction such as seminars, workshops, conferences and conventions. It is useful for addressing change and functional skills in context. Formal education is associated with schooling. It is planned and has long learning cycles which focus more on the theoretical.

Balance

Each type of leader requires a different optimal balance among these three kinds of delivery systems. For example, a Type I leader (small group leader) will be equipped largely through informal education with little nonformal education and probably no formal education related specifically to that small group ministry. A Type II leader (paraprofessional) will likely have an increasing amount of nonformal education and may begin some formal education related to his/her ministry. A Type III leader (e.g., full-time pastor of a single cell church) will likely have a decrease in nonformal education to facilitate an increase in formal education. Too often the informal education also declines during the equipping of a Type III leader. The formal education peaks and is generally nearly completed as a person begins to emerge as a Type IV leader (professional whose ministry is largely indirect). However, once again the nonformal and informal education begin to increase sharply. Type V leaders (national/international) experience a sharp increase in nonformal education and informal education for their equipping. Formal education is generally not appropriately available for them because of their busy schedules and already advanced educational level. The selection of the learners for the particular purpose and educational program is another equipping issue which requires careful attention.

To provide the wrong balance of an educational mix for a given type of leader may cause trouble for the leader or for the educational program in terms of nonacceptance. To evaluate the appropriateness of the balance one must look at the issues of the purpose of the educational program, what its goals are, its content, who is in control, the costs, the relevance of the education to the ministries of the leaders being taught and the timing (when in terms of life and ministry cycles). A change with any one of these variables will affect all of the others and the overall balance as well.

The actual equipping of emerging leaders falls on the shoulders of every church leader of every level. One is responsible for the equipping of others to fill his/her own responsibility— whether one is a Sunday School teacher, elder, pastor, agency administrator, or theological educator, the responsibility remains.

The equipping may take a variety of forms, but whatever the form, there must be a balance among the emphases on knowing, doing and becoming. Wholistic development is expected so the person will be complete, mature, fully equipped and competent.

One may see the equipping balance as requiring four interactive components: the inputs, ministry experience, dynamic reflection and spiritual formation. The inputs include the information and skills needed. The ministry experience includes all of the application of what is being learned in a real-life situation. The dynamic reflection provides the integration between the inputs, ministry experience and one's spiritual/ministry formation. The spiritual formation is the growing personal relationship with God as seen in the spiritual and ministry maturation processes. Each of these four elements contributes to the others and to the wholeness of an emerging leader's development. All four elements combine to provide the intentional base for spiritual leadership development.

The apostle Paul defines a leader's role in Eph 4:11 in terms of equipping. That word is variously translated from the Greek word *katartizo* as "equip," "teach," "mature," "bring to completion," "adjust," "fit together," and "perfect."

Contextualization of the Instruction

Equipping focuses the attention of the existing leader on contextualized instruction. It aims at fitting the person for ministry. *Katartizo* and the related word *ekartizo* suggest the idea of adjustment to fit the context. The existing leaders help tailor the emerging leader to fit the followers and ministry context according to the Lord's standards.

Paul's charge to Timothy to "correct, rebuke and encourage with great patience and careful instruction" (2 Ti 4:2) complements the purposes of Scripture (3:15–17) which result in a person being "thoroughly equipped for every good work." Timothy is to equip others so they will be able to meet the demands of every good work.

Every action that the leader takes or does not take is information about the leader's values and seriousness about those values.

> People around a leader are always alert to what he or she is doing. Although they attach importance to what leaders say, they will be truly impressed only by what leaders do . . . Their behavior . . . sends signals and messages about which behaviors are appropriate and acceptable and which are not.[22]

While not every leader is gifted as a teacher, the role of a leader includes the equipping of others for ministry. The equipping may be done in many ways. One may formally educate another in a school or informally enable through modeling. A planned nonformal approach may be designed in an apprenticeship or internship. The possible variations among these three contrastive educational modes stretch toward infinity. However, the most powerful educational form is that of deliberate modeling.

Modeling

The apostle Paul instructed three churches and Timothy to follow his example which included what he said and did.[23] He specifically spelled out to Timothy the issues to exemplify: speech, life, love, faith and purity. He exhorted him to model all of these issues so that everyone would see his progress (cf. 1 Ti 4:12–16). Jesus put it even more plainly when He said, "Follow me, and I will make you fishers of men" (Mk 1:17). The equipping, then, occurs in the following, imitating and participation of ministry. However, one must remember that growth can not be forced, only facilitated. It comes from within. We must provide a suitable stimulating context for the person to grow, but the choice—will to grow—comes from the emerging leader. The intended equipping-developmental process obviously aims to include all believers. Every believer is expected to develop spiritually and to exercise her/his spiritual gifts in ministry.

Modeling provides two important leadership functions. It provides a wide range of opportunities to instruct, mentor, and guide the developing leader. The example of a respected mentor carries a powerful impact to the developing leader not only in content and skills, but affective and spiritual formation as well. The second important feature of modeling is that the existing leaders are actually leading at the time. There is no simulation— it is the real thing. Leaders learn to lead best from leaders in a real situation, not from abstractions.

Encouraging

Effective gardeners cultivate the young plants to encourage and stimulate their growth. They take care so that other faster-growing plants do not overtake the young ones, shade them and stunt their growth. They  will watch and act as necessary to provide water, fertilizer, insecticides, herbicides, stakes and other care.

Barnabas (the Son of Encouragement) modeled this role for future generations of Christian leaders. While he deserved his nickname for many reasons, it especially applies in the encouraging sponsorship and cultivation of the apostle Paul. He risked his reputation to sponsor Paul's introduction and entry into the

Jerusalem church (Ac 9:27). The Jerusalem church leaders well remembered Paul's reputation with fear and distrust. Barnabas encouraged and stood firm, and Paul entered. Barnabas continued to encourage, mentor and instruct Paul. When they went to Cyprus, the people observed that Barnabas was in charge, but now Paul had become the spokesperson (cf. Ac 13:1–13, Paul and Barnabas in Cyprus). After leaving, Barnabas continued his growth-encouraging role by following Paul. No longer were they referred to as "Barnabas and Saul," but now as "Paul and Barnabas."

A key continuing role for existing leaders is the encouragement of emerging leaders. The encouragement may take the form of continuing attention to the context, sponsorship, modeling, instruction, protection, recognition of giftedness, or helping the emergent leader reflect and work through tests and challenges. The public legitimizing recognition of developing leaders which puts the existing leaders' status on the line for them serves both to empower and motivate.

Protection is an encouragement function which a leader-shepherd assumes for the people under his/her care. Emerging leaders are vulnerable to a number of predictable threats which the established leader must not only expect, but address. Criticism is certain to come. Someone said, "It is only a ship that is dead in the water that creates no waves." Criticism and resistance will arise as soon as the new leader begins to initiate structure or even show consideration. The older established leader can greatly help at this point both to protect and if need be to correct the emerging leader.

When Charles assumed the role of senior pastor, he recognized this important developmental function. He said to the people in the church, including the leaders, "If you have any criticism of my staff, make it to me."

Another encouragement-protection function is that of making space for emergence. A young plant can easily wither and die simply because it has no space in which to grow. Similarly, the emerging leaders may find it very hard to grow if the competition takes all of their energies. To keep up with the more developed or to compete for a significant space to grow may stunt the overall growth of the new leader. The established leader can assist or encourage by structuring the situations to free the new leader from unhealthy competition. The group size, group maturity, motivational level, task structure and new leaders' status and role all come under the watchful, protecting eye of the existing leaders. The aim is that everything in the situation will work for the good of the group and its purpose and for the ongoing development of the emerging leader.

To effectively encourage emerging leaders at least two ongoing processes are required: the recognition of their contributions and the celebration of their accomplishments.

Leaders should look even for small accomplishments to recognize and celebrate. The public celebration of accomplishments encourages not only the people who have made the accomplishments, but others as well. Kouzes and Posner assert on the basis of their research that "public ceremonies and rituals are the ingredients that crystallize personal commitment."[24]

Encouragement is what keeps younger leaders flourishing while the lack of it allows them to wither and die. The spiritual gift of exhortation carries the idea of standing alongside to encourage. One name given to the Holy Spirit by Jesus is Comforter—One who is called alongside to encourage.

A young plant is very vulnerable to heat, cold, drought, insects and other threats. Gardeners then take care to protect and facilitate its growth. Encouragement is particularly needed for younger leaders because they are most sensitive to criticism and ostracism.

Transitions

Leadership transition is a common feature of all leadership contexts. A leadership transition is an altered leadership situation in which the leader experiences a change in the influence means available to him/her, a shift in the value base on which he/she works and/or a change in the followers. Changes in influence means may result through the developmental process of increased cognitive development, skill development or spiritual formation. They may result from an altered organizational status/role. Transitions may also result from a shift in the kinds of power which are available to the leader. Spiritual leaders may expect transitions as they learn to appropriate spiritual power and as their spiritual authority increases.

A change in the value base will also lead to leadership transitions. A person may experience an inward change of values (conversion, back-sliding, paradigm shift). The person may move from one leadership situation to another where the values in the community or group are different.

Any change in the followers will likely precipitate a leadership transition. Followers change as they mature—ability, motivation, needs, perspectives all change, requiring the leader's adjustment. Different people may come under the leader's influence thus changing the leader's and followers' relations in the group.

Christian leaders are expected to be in transition (Eph 4:11–13). Leaders are expected to equip others. The equipping and selection of others continues throughout one's ministry. The personal transition of beginning to minister and then development are all transitional processes.

The leader's equipping of others will bring them to be like himself/herself. This very process then may place the followers in a position to compete with or to replace the older leader. If the followers move to other contexts, the transition continues.

Leadership transitions recur throughout the life of a leader. An emerging leader makes a number of transitions in every aspect of his/her leadership. Shifts in role and status are obvious. Growth in spiritual formation and ministry maturation bring transitions. One may experience shifts in terms of his/her sphere of influence or type of ministry, whether it be direct or indirect. Transitions arise through selection processes and through equipping processes. They may come because of death, termination, retirement, change of location or any one of many other kinds of reasons. Leadership transitions are a fact of life for leaders.

One may say that leaders are always in a state of transition and involved with others who are in transition. Some leaders, however, prepare for transitions and the emergence of others while other leaders do not. These two kinds of leaders are described well in a comparison between a banyan tree and a banana tree.

"Nothing grows under a banyan tree." This South Indian proverb speaks of leadership styles. The banyan is a great tree. It spreads its branches, drops air-roots, develops secondary trunks and covers the land. A full grown banyan may cover more than an acre of land. Birds, animals and humans find shelter under its shade. But nothing grows under its dense foliage, and when it dies, the ground beneath lies barren and scorched.

The banana tree is the opposite. Six months after it sprouts, small shoots appear around it. At 12 months a second circle of shoots appear beside the first ones, now six months old. At 18 months the main trunk bears bananas which nourish birds, animals and humans, and then it dies. But the first offspring are now full grown, and in six months they too bear fruit and die. The cycles continue unbroken as new sprouts emerge every six months, grow, give birth to more sprouts, bear fruit and die.[25]

Some leaders are like the banyan trees. They have great influence and their ministries are widely productive and beneficial. They, however, do not prepare for the transitions which will allow for the emergence of other leaders. They only equip followers, not leaders.

What is desired are leaders who allow the emergence of leaders even as they face personal transitions. What is needed are leaders who facilitate the transitions of others as they are emerging into leadership. This emergence is sometimes seen as threatening, but in the long term the people who equip others to be ready for the inevitable transitions are the leaders whose influence will remain and extend into future generations.

Existing leaders, then, recognizing their responsibilities to assist emerging leaders can assist in leadership transitions in several ways: selection, equipping, engagement/disengagement, and encouragement in transitional crises such as an abrupt assumption of responsibilities or a termination. The equipping of emerging leaders generally brings them into transitions. It may bring them into transitions which they did not expect. The more mature leaders should participate in the responsibility for the newer leaders to orient them to the transitional issues that their equipping is likely to bring. For example, advanced education often dislocates one socially and economically from one's former status and role relationships.

Engagement/Disengagement

One of the most difficult transitional issues to be faced by both the existing and emerging leaders centers on engagement and disengagement. The new leader is expected to engage in leadership as soon as his/her ability and motivation match the followers and situation. The existing leaders' task is to step aside while facilitating this engagement. Over-zealousness on the part of the emerging leader or a grasping on the part of an existing leader can seriously complicate the situation. Wise leaders not only anticipate, but facilitate this process.

Transplanting

Often a leader's most important ministry takes place in a very different context from where she/he began. While Paul's ministries in Antioch and Jerusalem were important, his greater contributions were in other places. While Barnabas contributed significantly to the church in Jerusalem, the Lord moved him on to Antioch and Cyprus.

As a gardener will transplant a young tree to where it can best please its owner by bearing fruit for him/her, the emergent leader is often transplanted to suit his "Owner." To facilitate this process, existing leaders may assist in the reassignment of people in ministry.

The transplanting is done with the qualities of the tree, the local situation, and the fruit-bearing goals of the owner in mind. By the time the transplanting occurs, the fruit-bearing potential should be clear. The context and followers should be considered to maximize the person's potential.

Existing leaders will give attention to the person in transition because in a very real sense the person is in the process of being uprooted. The familiar support networks of friends, associates and family have been disrupted. New supportive and nurturing relational networks have not yet been established. The person may feel the loss and may experience both exhilaration and depression. There may be a sense of frustrated confusion. One's sense of direction and self-image may be vulnerable at this time. The existing leaders then must give personal attention to the person in transition as well as to the situation into which the transition is being made. Existing leaders can either greatly facilitate transitions or make them very difficult. They can facilitate transition by helping the emerging leader take root. They can help build the relational networks, the legitimacy and the power base from which the emerging leader can function.

Leaders should expect to either be in transition themselves or assisting others in transition very frequently. This being involved in transition does not mean that one is changing jobs, but rather that growth is occurring where one is. Transitions occur whenever one's status or role changes. They may occur laterally or they may occur where significant changes result in the type of leadership and/or sphere of influence. Transitions occur when new personnel enter the scene. Transitions always occur when a person leaves.

Existing leaders serve under the direction of the Holy Spirit's direction in effecting the disciplining and growth directing processes of pruning. Existing leaders may participate in this process or the Spirit may initiate these processes outside the control of the existing leaders.

One time, much to my wife's consternation, I pruned a plant that badly needed pruning. However, I did not know the proper way to prune that kind of plant. The result was that the plant went into shock, struggled briefly and then died. Existing leaders must take care when they seek to initiate criticism, reproof, correction or disciplinary action because, as with pruning a plant, if it is done improperly the result may be impaired growth or even death. As the pruning of one branch will often stimulate an adjacent branch or neighboring tree to grow more rapidly, one must take care so that through the pruning process one does not actually put the branch being pruned at a disadvantage. The overall context (situation and followers at least) must be considered in the process.

Pruning

While suffering may serve other positive functions, it certainly does often serve a pruning function. One can not attribute all of a person's suffering to any personal fault or sin, rather, some suffering serves as a fire to test one's faith. Suffering may facilitate a kind of discipline which shapes one for growth or cuts away the superfluous growth. It may also stimulate the growth of the root system.[26]

Dysfunctions in Developing Leaders

The work of the Spirit clearly aims at the development of men and women as leaders even as they seek to train, equip or develop others. Were human sinfulness not to enter the picture, all would be well. However, the spiritual, social and cultural realities demonstrate that less than the ideal prevails.

Each of the positive ideals noted above for the existing leaders to do in the development of emerging leaders has a dysfunctional, counter-developmental or counterfeit side. Whenever an existing leader does not discern or follow God's leading through the Word and His Holy Spirit, the whole leadership development process begins to go awry. The wrong people will be selected by the wrong criteria for the wrong jobs or ministries. Rather than encouragement, discouragement will be the norm. The new leader will not be empowered, but will more likely experience alienation, impoverishment and isolation. Rather than growing to met high expectations, the emergent leader will shrivel into a passive anonymity.

To prevent these disruptive dysfunctions, the existing leaders must keep in touch with God's will through their own personal devotional life and study of the Word as it relates in their ministry context. The application to their ministry context must be developed whether it is in the Indonesian transmigration area with farmer-evangelists, in Berlin with the newly freed East Germans or with the gangs in South Central Los Angeles. The dysfunctions can only be prevented as the existing leaders continue to recognize that they too are "under development."

Summary

The existing leader's role reflects the work of the Holy Spirit. Existing leaders put hands, feet, voice and a face to the work of the Holy Spirit. Selection (recruitment), contextual preparation, ministry assignment, encouragement and equipping all fall in the existing leaders' role. These expectations for existing leaders apply to all leaders, not just apostles, prophets, evangelists, pastors and teachers (Mt 28:18–20; 2 Ti 2:2). Leaders must keep in touch with the Spirit to prevent serious dysfunctions for both their own lives and in the development of the others they are seeking to influence. The work of the Holy Spirit and of existing leaders, however, can be ineffective if the complementary role of the emergent leader is neglected in the development process.

Through all of the work of existing leaders three key sets of relationships must be not only maintained, but cultivated. The first is personal submissive obedience toward God. Discerning obedience is the goal. The second is with the existing congregation or Christian community being served. Cultivating the relationship with the community is a critical part of the role of the existing leaders. The Spirit does work in and through the community. Leaders serve a "priestly" function in representing the community. They speak not only "to" but "for" the community. Often leaders may discern the Spirit's leading through the community. For example, the church leaders discerned the Spirit's leading in the community to send Barnabas and Saul to Cyprus (Act 13:3). The Christian community should never be discounted as Christian leaders seek to discern that they may lead and lead others to lead. Since leadership is distributed widely in the church, any leader who tries to run solo is clearly neither discerning nor obedient.

The third key relationship is with the context or environment. Christian leaders must give attention to the environment in which they serve as stewards. It is not enough for the Spirit to work and for existing leaders to work. Emerging leaders must respond appropriately. The following chapter outlines the key responses expected of the emerging leader.

Through these three primary sets of relationships the existing leaders model what is expected for the emerging leader. Mentoring in and relationally empowering the emerging leader is a primary function of existing leaders. The potential for influence increases with the quality of the relationship. Quality relationships require time and shared experiences.

End Notes

1 The appropriate balance of the "priestly"—people's representative role, the "prophetic"—God's spokesperson role, and the "kingly"—administrative and protective roles must be kept when seeking to discern accurately God's will in a given situation with and for another person.

2 Bernard Bass, *Stogdill's Handbook of Leadership* (New York: The Free Press, 1981).

3 Paul Hersey and Kenneth H. Blanchard, *Management of Organizational Behavior Utilizing Human Resources,* Fifth edition (Englewood Cliffs, NJ: Prentice Hall, 1988).

4 Michael Youssef, *The Leadership Style of Jesus* (Wheaton: Victor Books, 1986), p.156.

5 See Kouzes and Posner 1987:242.

6 Kennon L. Callahan, *Effective Church Leadership: Building on the Twelve Keys* (New York: Harper and Row, 1990): 154.

7 See Callahan, 1990: 155.

8 Fiedler, 1980:242.

9 See Hersey and Blanchard, 1988:275–281.

10 Youssef, 1986:156.

11 Fiedler, 1980:242.

12 Fiedler, 1980:242.

13 Douglas W. Johnson, *The Care and Feeding of Volunteers* (Nashville: Abingdon, 1978):22–23, 41.

14 Kouzes and Posner, 1987:164.

15 Kouzes and Posner, 1987:165.

16 See Paul Sersey and Kenneth H. Blanchard, *Management of Organizational Behavior Utilizing Human Resources* (Fifth Edition) (Englewood Cliffs, NJ: Prentice Hall, 1988).

17 Richard Foster, *Sex, Love and Power* 1985:206.

18 Jack Hayford, "Church Growth Lectures," Fuller Theological Seminary, October 23-24, 1991.

19 For a balanced treatment of spiritual encounters including "power encounters" see Charles H. Kraft, "What Kind of Encounters Do We Need in Christian Witness?" *Evangelical Missions Quarterly* (July 1991): 258-265.

20 Jack Hayford, "Church Growth Lectures," Fuller Theological Seminary, October 23-24, 1991.

21 Kouzes and Posner, 1987:175.

22 Kouzes and Posner, 1987:198.

23 See Ph 3:17; 4:9; 1 Co 4:16; 11:1; 2 Th 3:7–10; 2 Ti 1:13.

24 Kouzes and Posner, 1987:263.

25 Paul G. Hiebert. "Banyan Trees and Banana Trees," *The Christian Leader* 53:3 (February 13, 1990): 24.

26 Suffering may serve other very important functions which are better described in other analogical terms. As the heat and drought stimulates a plant to send its roots deeper, so suffering may serve to stimulate depth in an emerging leader. However, as with other parts of this analogy, suffering carries a serious risk. It may result in death. Christian leaders can expect some suffering.

CHAPTER SEVEN

THE EMERGENT LEADER'S ROLE

> *Chung Kim and Chege Kamau had set the appointment with Pastor James. Chung Kim's first question was, "I believe that God wants me to serve him as a pastor." Chege Kamau added, "I am sensing God's call to be a teacher. What are the key things we must do to become effective leaders?"*

Paul told Agrippa, "I was not disobedient to the heavenly vision" (Ac 26:19). Abraham's obedience continues to stand as an example for believers (Gen 22:2–3). Joshua did all he was told to do by Moses (Jos 11:15). D. B. Towner well summarized the essential developmental elements for the emergent leader in his song, "Trust and Obey."[1] The beginning point for effective spiritual leadership is effective followership. Trust and obedience provide the essential stimulation for both spiritual and ministry maturation. The maturation process grows from one's new nature. A person should expect maturation to occur, but it requires active stimulation through trust and obedience.

Trust and obedience do not come naturally. A person learns both. If existing leaders want their disciples to have the optimal head start, then their modeling trust and obedience is critical. Trust is expressed toward one's superiors, accountability group, in oneself and/or toward one's followers. Whether one is emerging as a Type I or a Type V leader, these two responses remain essential. Without trust and obedience failure is assured.

Kouzes and Posner assert,

> The winning strategy for fostering collaboration is to
> cooperate first, and then practice reciprocity. This
> means setting the example for the behavior that you
> desire in others. It requires you to demonstrate your
> commitment and trustworthiness before asking for
> the same from someone else ... Leaders must
> demonstrate their willingness to trust the members of
> their teams first, before the team members can
> wholeheartedly put their fate into the leaders' hands.[2]

The key New Testament word for follower is disciple. Jesus
invited people to become his disciples. Disciples follow, learn
and apply what is learned to their lives in ways that others can
tell whom they follow. The Greek word *mathetes*, which is
translated "disciple," may also be translated as "pupil,"
"apprentice" or "adherent." The word occurs in both masculine
and feminine forms. *Mathetes* is the "usual word for apprentice."[3] It occurs at least 250 times in the New Testament.
Mathetes denotes the person who has attached himself to Jesus
as his Master.[4] The word leaves no question about "a personal
attachment which shapes the whole life of the one described as
mathetes, and which in its particularity leaves no doubt as to
who is deploying the formative power."[5] A disciple is a follower
who learns to be like the one he/she follows (cf. Lk 6:40).

The disciples of Jesus had a deep personal allegiance to
Jesus as a person. There is no hint that His teaching was a
source of strength after the crucifixion or that the disciples recognized their having an important legacy in the Word of Jesus.[6]
Rather, they saw their relationship in personal-follower perspective.

To be a leader one must first learn to be a follower. To continue to be a leader one must also continue to be a follower.
Followership also appears in the Scriptures as servanthood. A
servant or slave, *doulos,* is utterly accountable for obedience to
his master. A servant, *diakonos*, follows instructions particularly in regard to the task at hand. The servanthood of *huperetes*
particularly recognizes the authority of one's superior. The

servant, *leitourgos*, recognizes the organizational structure over him.

The Maa-speaking peoples of Kenya and Tanzania have a key word for leader which addresses another dimension of being a follower. The word, *olaiguanani*, is commonly translated "chief." However, the idea of chiefs was introduced by the British. The word could be better translated as "the one who discusses." The *olaiguanani* is the person who, after listening to everyone else's opinions and all of the debates around an issue, will stand and announce the group's consensus decision about an issue. After speaking, the others will say, "Yes, that is what we have decided." His skills are listening and discerning the issues and how they best suit the interests of the community. In a sense the Maa elder is a follower, but he gives structure to the decision as he shows consideration and respect for every person who has spoken.

Being a disciple or a learner will result in becoming like the one who is being followed. Character formation is a critical part of the discipling process. A person's influence potential is based on trustworthiness which emerges out of his/her character **and** competence. Learning as a disciple also suggests that one is learning to be competent both with the acquisition of knowledge and skills like the one being followed. Emerging leaders are expected to be able to do something, that is, to perform leadership behaviors such as coordinate, motivate, solve problems, plan, teach, and so forth. Discipleship then aims at developing both character and competence. The skills associated with one's giftedness are to be developed as one develops spiritual and ministry maturity.

The building of the essential character and competence in followers to facilitate their development of leaders may well be taught by modeling. The existing leader is still an emergent leader, and as an emergent leader he or she can model the key required responses and traits for the ones he or she is seeking to influence.

Trust

One essential follower response or trait is trust—trust in the Lord to influence through other leaders. The writer of Hebrews says, "Without faith it is impossible to please God, because anyone who comes to him must believe that he exists and that he rewards those who earnestly seek him" (11:6). A follower expresses trust in confidence, conviction and a commitment to the leaders and their vision. This trust provides stimulus for the follower's growth in influence potential. Trust is absolutely essential in the development of spiritual leaders. To be allocated or delegated trust one must know how to trust. To receive commitment one must demonstrate commitment. To generate conviction one must demonstrate conviction. To receive confidence one must show confidence in others. As the emerging leader learns about trust and commitment from his/her mentors, then this same trust and commitment can be modeled for his/her followers.

The trust in another person is not a blind commitment nor a means to build a hierarchical structure of domination and oppression. Rather, it should move toward reciprocal ministry as the existing leader also trusts in the emerging leader.

This trust or commitment generally proceeds through a series of developmental stages. David Krawthwol, et. al., in presenting a taxonomy of educational objectives in the affective domain, outline a sequence which describes the sequence of the trust or commitment described here. The taxonomy reflects a five-step process: receiving—the willingness to attend to or receive certain stimuli; responding—active involvement and participation; valuing—the worth of a thing, phenomenon, or behavior; organization—the organization interrelationship and ordering of values; characterization by a value or a value complex—the generalization and integration of a total worldview.[7]

The process moves from being willing to listen or receive instruction to having one's whole worldview characterized by the new values. With this change in worldview all of the person's life is understood in the light of these new values and all of a person's actions will be based on and reflect this altered (converted, transformed) worldview.

When one looks at the well-documented leaders' lives in the Scriptures, the issue of trust—faith, faithfulness, conviction, confidence and commitment—consistently stands out. Leaders in both the Old Testament and New Testament have this trait in common in both their emergence and service stages of development. The writer of Hebrews makes it plain, "Without faith it is impossible to please God" (He 11:6). Jesus underscored the principle of building on faithfulness when He said, "Whoever can be trusted with very little can also be trusted with much" (Lk 16:10–12). His parables of the Pounds and Talents further demonstrate this same principle (Lk 19:11–27 and Mt 25:14–30). The beginning requirement for the developing leader is faith.

Obedience

Faith and action can not be separated in one's response. James declares, "I will show you my faith by what I do" (Jas 2:18). When one looks at the emergence of the faithful leaders mentioned in Heb 11, their active obedience leaps into one's attention. The beginning activity for an emergent leader, then, is obedience. For one to remain as a spiritual leader obedience continues as a key requirement. Trustworthiness appears through obedience. Trustworthiness is expected of spiritual leaders. (2 Co 4:1–2, It is required of a steward that he be found faithful.) Trustworthiness may be seen in many contexts as integrity or character. One's trustworthiness or integrity will be tested at every ministry development stage in one way or another. In every case obedience to the Word and to God's clear guidance is expected. A clear biblical principle related to obedience is found in De 28:1–68. God blesses obedience while He curses disobedience. The principle remains true on the personal or societal level. Obedience is required for God's blessing.

Obedience is closely related to accountability. The emerging leader will not only recognize his/her accountability, but will seek to be able to account for his/her actions, learning and atti-

tudes. A growing accountability is an expected characteristic of
an emerging and later functioning leader. This accountability is
seen in the words translated as disciple and servant. Again, this
obedience is not aimed at the building of domineering tyrants,
rather it seeks to build servants. The leader is no less a servant
than the one who is following. To Americans in particular the
idea of being obedient in the church raises cultural hackles, but it
is nonetheless an expected part of one's discipleship development.

Jesus asked the question,

> "Why do you call me, 'Lord, Lord,' and do not do
> what I say? I will show you what he is like who
> comes to me and hears my words and puts them into
> practice. He is like a man building a house, who dug
> down deep and laid the foundation on rock. When a
> flood came, the torrent struck that house but could
> not shake it, because it was well built. But the one
> who hears my words and does not put them into
> practice is like a man who built a house on the
> ground without a foundation. The moment the torrent
> struck that house, it collapsed and its destruction was
> complete" (Lk 6:46-49).

The apostle Paul writes of the accountability we have as
trustees or stewards for the gospel to the church at Corinth.

> So then, men ought to regard us as servants of Christ
> and as those entrusted with the secret things of God.
> Now it is required that those who have been given a
> trust must prove faithful (1 Co 4:1-2).

Leaders are accountable for the effects of their influence and
will ultimately give account to God for it. The building of this
accountability begins as one is a newly emerging leader.
However, this accountability does not diminish with the process
of maturing. Rather, it grows. Obedience is not just an expected
characteristic of an emerging leader, but of every person regardless of his/her age or maturity. Leaders who remain accountable

are more likely to remain effective over a lifetime. Roles and status may change, but accountability remains required. The key biblical pictures of Christian leaders focus on the idea of accountability. The primary idea of servanthood is accountability. Jesus' question, "Why do you call me 'Lord, Lord' and do not do what I tell you?" underscores this truth. A brief review of the key words which are translated as servant show this focus: 1) *doulos*—A willing self-submitting accountable attitude toward another person; 2) *diaconos*—A willing acceptance of accountability for a task; 3) *hyperetes*—A willing acceptance to be accountable to the authority of another person; 4) *leitourgos*—A willing accountability to the organizational structure, the community; and, 5) *pais*—Accountability as a child being a learner and respectful.

Western leaders often mistakenly picture a shepherd as a person of power with the flock. This idea is unfortunately taken into the role of pastor. The word pastor comes from the Latin word which means shepherd. People who would live in a pastoral society would not make this mistake. The picture of a shepherd is also one of accountability. The people who watch the flocks are generally the younger men. They do not own the flocks, but rather care for them for their fathers and grand-fathers. This imagery is clear in 1 Pe 5:1-4 where elders are described as shepherds who are to be accountable to the "chief shepherd."

The word picture of a steward is easier to understand in terms of accountability and obedience. Stewards/trustees are always expected to be accountable to the owner for the trust given to them.

To whom are emerging leaders and mature leaders accountable? The answer is of course, God. However, this accountable obedience is demonstrated through accountable obedience to other spiritual leaders, namely, men and women God has raised up as superiors, peers and even followers. The Holy Spirit provides gifts of influence to many people and all are to benefit (be accountably obedient) to the exercise of these gifts. Some are gifted with exhortation and others teaching. Emerging and senior leaders remain accountable to God to be accountable to others. Even Peter was held to be accountable for his ethnocentrism.

Emerging leaders learn to demonstrate obedience in their accountability for their own calling and gifts which are to be used for the common good of the church. Emerging leaders are accountable for the mission of the church to seek and save the lost and then to nurture the found so they can also participate in seeking and finding the lost. Emerging leaders learn to be accountable for the way that they live regardless of their status in the groups where they find themselves.

Obedience and accountability contribute to the formation of trustworthiness in the emerging leader. As the trust in the emerging leader grows because of his/her trustworthiness the potential for influence will grow. Without trust even a person who is competent will not be able to lead. The emerging leader then must obey in an accountable way before expecting others to obey.

The emerging leader in becoming an existing leader continues to develop. In this development spiral a person has to be careful not to demand the trust or obedience of others. It can only rightfully be allocated by others. It may be earned or won, but not demanded. While on the one hand, trust and obedience are required for one to develop, the paradox is that the leader who assumes, aspires or grasps the power which would force another to comply is moving out of an obedient, trusting relationship with his/her Lord. Allegiance is to the Lord, not just to another person. However, when properly developed our obedience often will be seen in response to God's leading through others.

Within his/her obedience the emerging leader will give time to reflect on the experience he/she has been having. Without reflection experience may be of little use.

The opportunities for growth often threaten or test the emerging leader's potential in ways he/she can not imagine. The obedience of the moment may seem irrelevant to both the present and the future. It may be pure drudgery or seem useless. Remember the response of the fishermen as they let their net over the side one more time (Lk 5:4–7). Opportunities for growth often appear as tests. The tests allow the emerging leader to demonstrate the integrity of his/her commitment. Through these often very private and seemingly unimportant checks, the genuineness of one's heart intent appears. These tests can be expected in both positive and negative forms. The positive forms may be seen in opportunities for service. The negative forms may be temptations. Often these temptations will arise around money, pride or sexual issues.

The emergent leader's role, then, is trust and obedience. The trust and obedience is in the Lord's service, but carried out under the spiritual authority of existing leaders. The obedience begins with the level of maturity the emergent leader has, as can be seen both in his/her motivation and ability. Often these two characteristics of maturity will be challenged for growth in the spiritual task given. Even after significant formal training time for reflection and life maturity, Moses was challenged with the demands for both trust and obedience as he was called to lead.

The guided trust and obedience of David, Daniel, and Timothy illustrate the importance of these two essential principles in the formative phases of a leader's development.

As trust and obedience continue, the emerging leader's spirituality begins to mature. Within this spirituality several maturing characteristics or traits appear. Among these traits are the fruits of the Spirit, love, joy, peace, patience, kindness, goodness, faithfulness, gentleness and self-control. Trustworthiness and integrity are repeatedly demonstrated in whatever situation arises. One's confident ability to discern the Lord's leading for oneself from a study of God's Word, prayer, and interaction with other Christians will become increasingly apparent.

The growing spiritual maturation which emerges out of trust and obedience provides the basis for an emerging spiritual authority given by the Holy Spirit and effectiveness in ministry or leadership. Spiritual leadership emerges out of one's quality of life. This quality of life is first given by the Holy Spirit and then nurtured by both existing leaders and the emerging leaders themselves (1 Co 5:17).

By thrust and obedience or responsible discipleship/servanthood, emerging leaders may be empowered to lead. Their initial legitimacy will be established or authorized by existing leaders, while the Holy Spirit will empower their long-term ministry effectiveness through the development and recognition of their spiritual authority. Emerging leaders do not passively receive this empowering, authorizing legitimacy to lead, but actively cooperate with existing leaders in serving in accordance with the gifts given by the Holy Spirit.

Through trust and obedience an emerging leader builds his/her leadership potential. Leadership potential is a combination of trustworthiness and competence as perceived by the people who are to be influenced. One's influence potential rests on the relationships of the person in that situation with all who are to be influenced. Three kinds of influence potential or power are required—spiritual, personal and "corporate." As the emerging leader trusts and demonstrates obedience in a situation relationships are developed which provide the essential power bases. Trust is established through which the power may be exercised. And, the emerging leader's competence develops. This competence is a combination of knowledge and skills plus the value based wisdom to apply them.

Summary

The individual roles of the Holy Spirit, existing leaders and emerging leaders all contribute essential elements to the development of emerging leaders. These three crucial leadership development roles continue in a local church, seminary or church agency regardless of its size or cultural setting. The Holy Spirit guides through the Word, other leaders and increasingly in the life of the emergent leader. The existing leaders, regardless of their gifts, are charged with leading in ways by which the new leader will mature internally in spiritual formation and externally in ministering. Existing leaders aid in discerning the Lord's will, preparing the context, making ministry assignments, encouraging, protecting, assisting in transition, teaching and shepherding the newer leader. The emergent leader's role is to mature, grow, and develop in the context of trusting obedience.

It is the nature of the plant to grow, mature and bear fruit for multiplication. Similarly, one should expect emerging leaders to develop and bear fruit. Spiritual leadership or that process influencing God's people toward His purpose should be facilitated by each of the gifts the Lord gives. That influence potential should be facilitated and expected to develop in the life of each Christian.

Non-growth in a plant indicates a pathological condition which should be addressed. As in a gardening situation, the problem may be with the plant, the soil, the climate, parasites or a host of other possibilities. Similarly, in the life of a Christian non-growth is not normal and should be addressed. Training is only one of many possible treatments and is not always appropriate. Training may increase leadership fruitfulness, but other issues (such as the context and followers) may have to be addressed first.

One can provide a stimulating medium for growth externally, but growth results from internal processes. A characteristic of the new nature of a Christian is to grow. Normal developmental growth should be expected, but it can not be forced. It can only be facilitated.

As a tree is nourished by its roots in the context where it grows, so also a Christian leader develops and grows in spiritual maturity as she/he interacts within the church. It is a transactional context in which the leader and the followers benefit from the interactions. Both one's mentors and followers provide the stimulus for continued growth and development. The nutrients for this growth come from the Holy Spirit through the Word and His personal ministries.

Likewise, as a tree gives stability to the soil/context where it grows, so also spiritual leaders contribute to the context where they serve. Leaders will not only benefit their immediate followers, but the wider context in which they all live and serve as well. In fact, for both long-term and optimal effectiveness the wise leader will seek to transform the context.

Wise nursery workers work with many kinds of trees and other plants which are at many stages of development at the same time. They will regularly plant seed and at the same time be caring for both young and mature trees. A pastor or existing church leader similarly will continually be involved in the development of a wide variety of spiritual leaders at every stage of the process. One seldom begins just at the beginning "planting" stage, but is rather involved with all of the stages simultaneously with different people in the church.

Spiritual leadership is not a narrowly limited set of functions, but is expected from every believer. Just as every person receives at least one "spiritual gift" so every person is expected to use it to influence others (lead) toward God's purposes. Every person is expected then to trust and obey to emerge into the role of influence God has prepared (Eph 2:10).

End Notes

1   "When we walk with the Lord in the light of His Word, What a glory He sheds on our way! While we do His good will, He abides with us still. And with all who will trust and obey. Trust and obey, For there's no other way, To be happy in Jesus but to trust and obey."

2   Kouzes and Posner, 1987:141.

3   See Rengstorf, 1967:IV:416.

4   Rengstorf, 1967:IV:441.

5   Rengstorf, 1967:IV:441.

6   See Rengstorf, 1967:IV:446.

7   David R. Krawthwol, et. al., *Taxonomy of Educational Objectives: The Classification of Educational Goals Handbook II: Affective Domain* (New York: David McKay Company, Inc. 1964).

CHAPTER EIGHT

SUMMARY AND RECOMMENDATIONS

This book has aimed at providing you a set of perspectives to initiate intentional leadership development in the church. While it is important to understand something about leadership theory, the roles of the Holy Spirit and of emerging leaders, you are the one who has been charged with the development of others. As an existing and informed leader, you need to fit five sets of concerns together to develop emerging leaders effectively. These five sets of concerns center around 1) the leader, 2) the followers, 3) the situation in which they interact, 4) the means of influence available to the leader(s) and followers, and, 5) the values affecting the leader(s), followers and situation. These five sets of concerns apply to every type of leader, ranging from the local volunteer substitute teacher of a small group to senior denominational, agency and international church leaders.

To fit these five concerns together initially requires discernment and then courage, faith and the whole range of leadership functions in a context of integrity. These functions were mentioned briefly earlier in the book.

The Leader

When looking at the emerging leader with a view to taking initiative for development, five issues require clear discernment: 1) The leader's calling. What is God calling the person to be and to do? 2) The leader's competence. Both the leaders' present and potential competence in terms of knowledge, attitudes and skills requires a discerning assessment. 3) The leader's character or spiritual maturation. Successful ministry development assignment begins with and depends on an accurate assessment of the person's spiritual or ministry maturity.[1] 4) The commitment of the emerging leader. What motivates the person as a leader? What is the driving vision? 5) The emerging leader's relationships. The present status and role as well as the quality of relationships with God, followers, peers, superiors and in the broader context will all affect the development of the emerging leader. A discerning assessment of these five concerns will provide a strong base on which to begin to build leadership development.

The Followers

Effective leadership development requires an accurate discernment of the present or projected followers of the emerging leader. At least three concerns require attention: 1) their abilities to carry out the task at hand, 2) their motivation to accomplish the task at hand, and 3) the quality of their relationships with God, the emerging leader, among themselves and with others in their broader context. The person who aims to equip leaders without discerning these concerns for their followers will not likely be effective in the long run.

The Situation

Discernment of the leadership situation is also a key component for the person who would develop others as leaders. Three levels of situational discernment greatly enhance the formation of effective leadership development: 1) worldview, 2) culture and 3) the task at hand.

One's worldview is the set of undergirding assumptions which serve to explain and give coherence to all of a person's values and behaviors. One's worldview, while very personal, is also shared. It is out of a shared worldview that culture emerges.

The culture which needs to be discerned includes both the culture of the community and the organization in which the emerging leader will serve. Questions of forms and functions in that setting require discernment.

Thirdly, as one who is concerned about the development of others as leaders, a clear understanding of their task or job will provide a useful base on which to begin designing a training approach. What is the task? How is it structured? What are the priorities? What competencies are required for the task?[2]

A clear understanding of the situation provides guidance for the leader developer not only in terms of what to do with and for the emerging leader, but what must be done in the situation to facilitate the emergence of the new leader.

Influence Means

Three different kinds of influence means are typically available to an emerging spiritual leader. To develop a person as a leader requires careful discernment on the part of the trainer of each one. The three types of influence include personal, corporate or community, and spiritual. The use of power is involved in each. The right to use power, that is, authority, is involved in each type of influence. Each of the three kinds of influence interact and affect the leader, the followers and the situation.

Discerning personal means of influence requires attention to a person's individual behaviors as well as to the patterned behavior which is commonly called one's leadership style. Each emerging leader has a distinctive set of personal traits and relationships which provide a personal power base. The discernment of this power base and the rights which are given by superiors, peers and subordinates to use it allows the leadership developer to know both the initial constraints and facilitating elements on which to build.

Understanding the corporate or community influence means in which the emerging leader will serve provides key perspectives to both development and ministry assignment. The community or corporate means provide shared structures, policies, practices, and procedures which are generally beyond the control of the emerging leader. The new leader must fit in to be effective. A clear discernment of the leader and the situation will greatly assist you as the trainer or developer both in fitting the person to the situation and knowing how to equip the person for that situation.

The discerning of the spiritual means of influence available in the person and situation provides a key to both the selection and equipping of leaders in that context. A careful discernment of the emerging leader's spiritual maturity will provide clues about the spiritual authority available. A discernment of the community to be led will provide essential insight into their spirituality, spiritual power and intercessory undergirding of the emerging leader. A discernment of the context where the emerging leader will serve will provide clues about the level of spiritual warfare in the community.

Values

An understanding of three different value bases provides the foundation on which the overall spiritual leadership development approach must be built. These three foundational value bases include: 1) the revealed values found in the Scriptures, 2) the values of the community to be served, and 3) the values of the person who is being trained.

The normative values come from the revealed ones in Scripture. The community values should be honored as long as they do not conflict with Scripture. The personal values may need orientation or adjustment first toward Scripture and then secondly toward the local situation.

These value bases serve both to constrain and guide the training. They also provide some of the essential content of the developmental training.

Growing Leaders at Home

Five general recommendations summarize what has been advocated in this book.

1.	Every leader must see as an essential part of his/her role the development of other leaders.

Every leader—whether that leader is a Sunday school teacher, elder, preacher, organist, usher, worship leader or seminary professor—should be developing others both as replacements and as an equipped core for multiplication. The developing and empowering of others not only demonstrates obedience, but will provide the basis for future growth.

The development I am recommending includes the preparation of the context, ministry assignment, encouragement, equipping, discipline, and assisting in transitions.

> 2. Every new believer should be helped to understand that to accept Jesus as Lord is to accept ministry responsibility in His body, the Church.

Passivity among church members too often is both encouraged and taught by the existing leaders. Pastors, elders, deacons, worship leaders, ushers and others are too often jealous of their position and status. We must not be afraid for others to be equipped to replace us and then to let them replace us. Grace is free, but too often we have made it cheap. Discipleship begins with conversion. We need to put aside our pride and fear. We need to place people in simple growth-stimulating ministries from the time of their conversion.

To wait weeks or months allows the seeds of nominality to sprout and take root.

> 3. Recognize and support the distribution of leaders.

At least 10% of a growing church will be Type I leaders. A healthy church will have 2–3% of its members as Type II leaders and at least .5–1% of its members will emerge as Type III leaders. Churches over 250 members will likely have at least one Type IV leader and as they grow beyond 600–700 they may have several Type IV leaders.

Another side of recognizing and supporting a distributed leadership embraces the biblical teaching of spiritual gifts. While each one serves in the church, each one is also served. No one is outside of the body or its functions. Each one serves for the good of the whole. The pastor, for example, continues to receive teaching, encouragement, counsel and hospitality even as the elders continue to receive exhortation and teaching. They receive even as they give. I am not advocating any particular cultural model, but rather a set of principles. These principles apply regardless of local church polity.

> 4.   Give special attention to multiplying Type I
>   leaders.

They are the key to the present and future spiritual, organic and numerical growth of the church. They need to be encouraged, recognized, honored and given the special equipping they need to function. Many are gifted to serve in a wide range of Type I leadership roles and ministries.

The job is well described by the apostle Paul in the word *katartizo*—equip them, adjust their ministries, fit them together, perfect them for ministry.

> 5.   Remember we are to be *Christian* leaders.

We are under Christ's authority. We are to use His power, that is, the power of the Holy Spirit. We lead to accomplish His purpose. We are to obediently lead only to bring people to Christ and to lead them to be fully obedient to all Christ commanded. We have the right to influence—the authority—only to do as our Lord commanded. Let's do it!

End Notes

1   One useful theoretical perspective has been developed by J. Robert Clinton in his *Leadership Emergence Theory* (1989).

2   Robert F. Mager and Kenneth M. Beach, Jr., have designed a very useful little book entitled *Developing Vocational Instruction* (Belmont, CA: Fearon-Pitman Publishers, Inc. 1967), which provides a useful approach to understanding both the task at hand and its relationship to a training approach.

BIBLIOGRAPHY

Badaracco Jr., Joseph L. and Richard R. Ellsworth

    1989   *The Quest for Integrity in Leadership.* Boston: Harvard Business School Press.

Barclay, William

    1974   *Educational Ideals in the Ancient World.* Grand Rapids: Baker Book House.

Bass, Bernard

    1981   *Stogdill's Handbook of Leadership.* New York: The Free Press.

Bauer, Walter

    1957   *A Greek-English Lexicon of the New Testament and Other Early Christian Literature.* Translated and adapted by William F. Arndt and F. Wilbur Gingrich, Chicago: The University of Chicago Press.

Bennett, David W.

    1989   "Images of Emergent Leaders: An Analysis of Terms Used by Jesus to Describe the Twelve." Unpublished manuscript, March.

Blake, R. R. and J. S. Mouton

    1964   *The Managerial Grid.* Houston: Gulf.

Burns, J. M.

    1978   *Leadership.* New York: Harper and Row.

Clinton, J. Robert

  1984   *Leadership Training Models Manual.* Unpublished manuscript.

  1986   "Leadership Emergence Patterns." Unpublished manuscript.

Clinton, J. Robert (cont.)

  1988   *The Making of a Leader.* Colorado Springs: Nav-Press.

  1989   *Leadership Emergence Theory.* Altadena, CA: Barnabas Resources.

Conn, Harvie M. and Samuel F. Rowen (eds.)

  1984   *Missions and Theological Education in World Perspective.* Farmington, MI: Associates of Urbanus.

Deaton, Charles and Michael MacCaskey

  1978   *All About Pruning.* San Francisco: Ortho Books.

Drucker, Peter F.

  1968   "Leadership: More Doing Than Dash." *Wall Street Journal,* January 6.

Elliston, Edgar J.

  1981   "Biblical Criteria for Christian Leadership." In *Curriculum Foundations for Leadership Education in the Samburu Christian Community.* Ph.D. Dissertation, Michigan State University, 1981. pp. 187–226.

  1985   "Developing Christian Leaders." Address presented to the Pan-African Conference of Christian Church/ Church of Christ Missionaries, Nairobi, Kenya. July. pp. 1–2.

  1989   *Christian Relief and Development: Training Leaders for Effective Ministry.* Dallas: Word Books.

Elliston, Edgar J. and W. Michael Smith

1976   "An Outline for Program Planning and Evaluation,"
        Unpublished manuscript.

Fiedler, Fred E.

1967   *A Theory of Leadership Effectiveness.* New York:
        McGraw Hill.

1980   "The Trouble with Leadership Training is that it
        Doesn't Train Leaders," In William R. Lassey and
        Richard R. Fernandez, *Leadership and Social
        Change.* La Jolla, CA: University Associates.
        pp. 238–246.

Findlay, G. G.

1961   "St. Paul's First Epistle to the Corinthians." In W.
        Robertson Nicoll (ed.), *The Expositors' Greek
        Testament.* 2:729–953. Grand Rapids: William B.
        Eerdmans Publishing Company.

Gerber, Virgil

1980   *Discipling Through Theological Education by Exten-
        sion.* Chicago: Moody Press.

Greenslade, Philip

1984   *Leadership, Greatness and Servanthood.* Minneapo-
        lis: Bethany House Publishers.

Hayford, Jack

1991   "Church Growth Lectures," Fuller Theological Semi-
        nary. Oct 23-24.

Hersey, Paul and Kenneth H. Blanchard

1988   *Management of Organizational Behavior Utilizing
        Human Resources.* Fifth edition. Englewood Cliffs,
        NJ: Prentice Hall.

Hiebert, Paul G.

1990   "Banyan Trees and Banana Trees." *The Christian Leader,* 53:3 (February 13):24, .

Hollander, Edwin

1978   *Leadership Dynamics.* New York: The Free Press.

House, Robert J.

1971   "A Path-Goal Theory of Leader Effectiveness." *Administrative Science Quarterly* 16:321–338.

Johnson, Douglas W.

1978   *The Care and Feeding of Volunteers.* Nashville: Abingdon.

Kirkpatrick, John

1988   *A Theology of Servant Leadership.* D. Miss. dissertation, Fuller Theological Seminary.

Kittel, Gerhard

1967   *Theological Dictionary of the New Testament.* Translated by Geoffrey W. Bromiley. Grand Rapids: William B. Eerdmans Publishing Company.

Knox, John

1956   "The Ministry in the Early Church," In H. Richard Niebuhr and Daniel D. Williams (eds), *The Ministry in Historical Perspective.* New York: Harper and Row. p. 21.

Kouzes, James M. and Barry Z. Posner

1987   *The Leadership Challenge: How to Get Extraordinary Things Done in Organizations.* San Francisco: Jossey-Bass Publishers.

Kraft, Charles

1979   *Christianity and Culture.* Maryknoll, NY: Orbis.

1991   "What Kind of Encounters Do We Need in Our Christian Witness?" *Evangelical Missions Quarterly* 27:3 (July): 258-268.

Krawthwol, David R., et. al.

1964   *Taxonomy of Educational Objectives: The Classification of Educational Goals Handbook II: Affective Domain.* New York: David McKay Company, Inc.

Lassey, William R. and Richard R. Fernandez

1976   *Leadership and Social Change.* La Jolla, CA: University Associates.

Mager, Robert F. and Kenneth M. Beach, Jr.

1967   *Developing Vocational Instruction.* Belmont, CA: Fearon Pitman Publishers, Inc.

McGavran, Donald A. and Win Arn

1974   *How to Grow A Church.* Glendale, CA: Regal.

McKinney, Lois

1980   "Training Leaders," In Virgil Gerber, *Discipling Through Theological Education by Extension.* Chicago: Moody Press.

Nicoll, W. Robertson (ed.)

1961   *The Expositors' Greek New Testament.* Grand Rapids: William B. Eerdmans Publishing Company.

Niebuhr, H. Richard and Daniel D. Williams (eds.)

1956   *The Ministry in Historical Perspective.* New York: Harper and Row.

Peters, Thomas J. and Robert H. Waterman, Jr.

1982   *In Search of Excellence*. New York: Warner Books.

Rambo, David

1981   "Patterns of Bible Institute Training Overseas,"
        "Theological Education by Extension: What is it
        Accomplishing?" "Crisis at the Top: Training High
        Level Leaders," *Leadership for the Cities: Facing the
        Urban Mandate*, 1981 Church Growth Lectures,
        Fuller Theological Seminary.

Rengstorf, K. H.

1967   *"Mathetes."* In Gerhard Kittel, *Theological Dictio-
        nary of the New Testament*. Translated by Geoffrey
        W. Bromiley. Grand Rapids: William B. Eerdmans
        Publishing Company.

Richards, Lawrence O.

1975   *A Theology of Christian Education*. Grand Rapids:
        Zondervan Publishing House. 1975.

Shartle, C. L.

1956   *Executive Performance and Leadership*. Englewood
        Cliffs, NJ: Prentice Hall.

Tyler, Ralph

1950   *Basic Principles of Curriculum and Instruction*.
        Chicago: University of Chicago Press.

Ward, Ted

1984   "Servants, Leaders and Tyrants." In *Missions and
        Theological Education in World Perspective*. Harvie
        M. Conn and Samuel F. Rowen (eds.). Farmington,
        MI: Associates of Urbanus.

1977   "Facing Educational Issues." In *Church Leadership Development*. Glen Ellyn, IL: Scripture Press Ministries.

Wrong, Dennis H.

1980   *Power—Its Forms, Bases and Uses*. New York: Harper and Row.

Youssef, Michael

1986   *The Leadership Style of Jesus*. Wheaton: Victor Books.

Yukl, Gary A.

1989   *Leadership in Organizations*. 2d ed. Englewood Cliffs, NJ: Prentice Hall.